A
Positive
Contribution

Chris Buss

First published in the United Kingdom in 2008
by 70up Publishing

ISBN 978-0-9559058-0-3

Printed and bound in Great Britain

CONTENTS

Page:	Section.
1	Foreword
4	In the Beginning
7	The Early years. 1908-1918
14.	The Twenties and Thirties 1918-1938
31.	The coming of War and the War 1938-1945
48.	After the War 1945-55
69.	The late Fifties 1955-61
90	The Sixties 1961-69
114	The Seventies 1970-1980
132	The early Eighties 1980-84
139	Late Nineteen Eighties 1984-89
153	The Nineties 1990-1999
174	The new Millenium 2000-2008
191	Postscript...A positive contribution
198	Appendices 1- Officers and Life boy Leaders of the 70th 2- NCO's of the 70th 3- Company strength 1908-2007 4-Competition Successes 5-Terminology

FOREWORD

100 years in the great scheme of things may not seem a long time, however, in starting to write this centenary account of the story of the 70th London Company of The Boys' Brigade, I have attempted to write an honest account of the men, boys and women that have served as officers , staff and members of the Company and have shaped thelives of members past as well as the present. For those unaquainted with The Boys' Brigade you may wish to aquaint your-self with the terminology section in Appendix 5 before reading fur-ther.

The activities and events that have occurred have been placed where possible into a wider context within the local area, the wider work of The Boys' Brigade and the world at large. Any such story will by definition be incomplete, particularly one which for its early years is reliant upon narrative accounts from members who have passed on or on limited written records. The writer has tried wherever possible to double check facts and events with original sources in particular the minutes of officers and NCO's meetings, battalion council min-utes, church and deacons meetings records, captain's annual reports and company newsletters but it has not always been possible to do this on a consistent basis. I have also avoided wherever possible from giving a personal slant on events trying to recount the facts as they are stated either by the person concerned or the written record.

I am indebted to the fiftieth anniversary account of the Company written by Ken Hill in 1958 and parts of that earlier account are included in this longer narrative. I would also like to thank those Old Boys who were interviewed or who completed questionnaires and have enabled this story to reflect a number of different views of life in the Company.

I would like to thank in particular Peter Clark , Arthur Bowbeer , Moreen and Percy Sore who have checked the accuracy of the account, corrected the grammar and spelling and generally assisted

in making this a true account of the first hundred years of the 70th

London.

I would also like to thank my wife Jennifer and my family for putting up with me writing this account as well as their patience and tolerance over the past twenty five years whilst I have been out on many an evening and weekend on Brigade business.

It is hoped you will enjoy this account of the first one hundred years of the 70th London Company of the Boys' Brigade.

Finally , I would like to thank the Local Heritage Initiative whose funding made this publication possible.

Chris Buss- April 2008

DEDICATION

This book is dedicated:

To the memory of William Cotsell founder captain of the 70th London Company , without whom the 70th would not have existed

To Bert Porter and Arthur Bowbeer who both continued the work as captain and have now received a higher reward.

To Peter Knights and Neil Pheasant who continued the high standards of the 70th in their time as captain

To all the other officers who have made the 70th the unique company that it has been and

To Barry Green and Jim Ballard without whom 90 years would not have reached 100.

THE BOYS' BRIGADE.

South London _____ BATTALION.

ENROLMENT OF COMPANY.

94 Paternoster Row. EC

December. 15th 19 0 8

W. E H Cotrell Esq
80 Manville Road, Tooting Common, SW

SIR,

       I am instructed by the BATTALION COUNCIL to inform you that they have enrolled your Company under the designation of the

70th London _____ COMPANY, THE BOYS' BRIGADE,

in connection with *Tooting Junction Baptist Church.* _____,

and have approved of the Appointment of the undernoted Gentlemen as Officers of said

Company, in accordance with your Application dated *Dec. 9th 1908* _____.

NAMES OF OFFICERS.

Captain.	William. E H Cotrell	3rd Lieut.	Clifford A. Blaydell
Chaplain.	Rev. J Kenningham	4th Lieut.	
1st Lieut.	Fredk. W Taylor	5th Lieut.	
2nd Lieut.	Ralph Harrop	6th Lieut.	

I have the honour to be,

Enclosures :   SIR,

_____

_____

Your obedient Servant,

Reg S Hancock

Battalion Secretary.

500 A. 9/05.

3

THE BEGINNING

Why was the 70th started in 1908 and who was the prime mover behind it? This question is difficult to answer. However, we do know that the Boys' Brigade (BB) was in its 25th year nationally in 1908, having been founded by William Smith in Glasgow in October 1883. Although the organisation spread rapidly across the United Kingdom and into the then British Empire, it had a slow start in the Tooting area , which had seen its first company start in 1905 with the 27th London based at the Fairlight Mission in Fairlight Rd. Amongst the four officers in that company were three brothers William, Herbert and Henry Cotsell. The brothers Cotsell lived at 80 Manville Rd off of Tooting Bec Common. William was the eldest of this particular group but they were part of a family of eleven (8 boys 3 girls) and were in membership of Trinity Rd Chapel. It is not known how the Cotsells had become interested in The Boys' Brigade, as they had, apparently not been members as boys, as there is no record of a company being in existence in the Alma Rd area of Wandsworth where they lived whilst they were growing up. We also do not know why they started with the 27th at Fairlight Hall rather than at Trinity Rd . However, Herbert Cotsell started the 37th London at Trinity Rd Chapel in 1908 leaving William and Henry with the 27th at Fairlight Hall.

Tooting in Edwardian times was very much socially a mixed community, the area between Mitcham Rd and Tooting Bec was just being developed with new working class accommodation being built by the London County Council. The houses in Longley Rd itself were larger and two were occupied by the famous musical hall stars of the day Harry Tate and Sir Harry Lauder. Travel was by tram or steam train from Tooting Junction Station - Yes there was a junction and the Northern Line tube was not to reach Tooting until 1926. Both ends of Longley Rd had a parade of small shops with names of traders long gone. It was in this area that the idea of a BB company was promoted.

The first sign of any interest in starting a Boys' Brigade company from within Tooting Junction Baptist church , Longley Rd was at the March 1908 deacon's meeting when one the deacons Mr. Ibbotson, the church treasurer, suggested that the church should start a BB company. The church at that time had just completed a major project to build a sanctuary to seat 700 people on the site of what is now Abingdon Court at the corner of Bickersteth Road and Longley Road. What prompted the idea of starting a BB company is not known. However by the summer of 1908 the church was in discussion with William Cotsell concerning starting a company . The approach in the first instance coming from the church, the deacons met with William Cotsell in October when he explained the working of the Brigade and that it was in his words "essentially a religious institution." It was proposed to promote the Company by a magic lantern talk to boys on the 10th November 1908 and that it would require 10 guineas to finance the Company through its first session (that's just under £900 at 2007 prices). The church as a whole were informed of the creation of the company on 18th November 1908. Application for registration was made with the London District on December 9th and the Company was registered on December 15th by the London Secretary - Roger Peacock . In addition to William Cotsell as Captain the other officers on the enrolment certificate were Frank Taylor, Ralph Harrup and Clifford Blazdell who were all church members, however the Brigade national records omit Clifford Blazdell and Frank Taylor on the record of Officers and add yet another Cotsell brother Frederick as the first Officers of the Company. The apparent discrepancy is probably due to the fact that the Company's first annual return at a national level would not have been made until the 1909-10 session at which time the District records correspond with the National records. The company was designated the 70th London Company, a designation used at least once previously for a company that was attached to Westminster Chapel in the early 1900's.

The Company's early meetings were split over three sites, but the primary meeting was for drill parade at 8.15pm on a Wednesday, initially at Sellincourt Rd school, a short walk from the church.However in some years Franciscan Rd school was used instead. Bible class was initially held in the Church parlour at 10.00am on Sundays whilst other meetings were held at the old brick & iron chapel buildings on what is now the site of 122/124 Longley Rd. This included from 1911 a clubroom on a Saturday night. In addition a fife band was started. The BB was not the only youth organisation in the area for 12-17 year old boys as there was a thriving Boys' Life Brigade at the Congregational Church at the end of Rookstone Rd, which coincidentally used Sellincourt School on a Monday night, and the scouts were just starting nationwide. However unlike its early namesake this 70th London, despite some early knocks, took root and grew.

First known photograph of the Company in 1910.

The Early Years. 1908-1918

Our knowledge of the early years of the Company is limited to the written records of old members, some central records held by the Brigade at London and national level and the occasional reference in church minute books as no other written records exist for the period before 1938. In the period up to the First World War it would seem that a routine pattern of regular meetings was adopted that with a little variation became the norm for the Company for most of the next 100 years. Bible Class on a Sunday, parade nights ,badge classes, band night during the week and sporting activities on a Saturday. In its early years the band was a flute (or fife) and drum band moving to a bugle band in 1912. The first record of a company football team was in 1910 when swimming and signalling classes also started. At the end of its first session 15 boys, just under half the Company strength, attended camp where the Cotsell family connection was strong with the 27th and 37th London Companies .The camp was at Goring, near Worthing between July 24th and August 1st 1909. In total 65 boys and 10 Officers attended from the three Companies. The Company, as previously mentioned, appears to have lost two Officers in its first session, and by 1914 both Ralph Harrup and Frederick Cotsell had resigned, leaving William Cotsell to run the Company single handed in terms of enrolled Officers throughout the period of the First World War.

Off to Camp 1910

Top: Camp Inspection 1910
Bottom: Band Practice 1911

Writing in 1978 one of the Company's founder members Frank Hysom, number 31 on the Company roll, writes about life as a boy in the 70th before the First World War.

"I do not remember missing a single Drill or Bible Class meeting ..... we met in the old tin building, with the small hall at the back.   Sgt. Adair taught us to be side drummers and play B flat flutes, playing 'Scipio' and 'Barren rocks of Aden'. Before we moved to Sellincourt Rd School we made the roof of the old hall resound. Mr Cotsell pro-vided up to date cleaning materials for the drums. Metal containers for the brass polish , then meths to finish it off. Just like everything he did -efficient On one occasion I went with Captain Cotsell to col-lect a new drum at Kennington and when coming back on the tram I was unwell, so we finished up coming home in a cab. The overall impression remains, that the organization, particularly of the Camp, bore the stamp of efficiency.   It was not all sports, or lounging about. At one Camp I recall the enjoyable Church Parade at Goring Parish Church. We once found a body on the beach. It was a fisher-man whose boat had overturned: it was my first, but by no means my last, experience of death. On our first camp before the onset of torrential rain we were instructed in the method of cutting a drain moat around tents to prevent water seepage into the tent floor. Then as we got into our blankets and groundsheets -all provided - Mr. Cotsell and his brother came round and literally sewed us in the groundsheets with cord to keep us from the wet ground."
Whilst talking of Camp, 1914 this time, Frank said: "I was success-ful in winning the mile walk - and was awarded a collar-box, for stiff collars." However , camp in 1914 was curtailed because as Frank said " 1914 camp was of course memorable, the War depart-ment recalled canvas and equipment hired from it, we struck camp early and went home" Frank, later, having joined the Army, under-age as many did, quickly became a L/Cpl., because he understood drill, and found himself marching in the 'Non-Conformist' Church Parade into Shoreham-by-Sea Baptist Church, only a few miles from his boyhood campsite.

Many of Frank Hysom's thoughts were shared by Fred Thomas who joined the company in 1914. Fred wrote the following back in 1988.

"The Company had been in existence only six years when in 1914, I joined. In those days you had to be 12 to join. There was no Junior Section and you were 'on probation' for the first three months. Discipline was strict and uniform consisted of pillbox hat, haversack and belt - which had to be perfect. The braid on the hat had to be blancoed, the haversack lily white (good old mum,) and its brass runners shining like the buckle on the belt.

"One always wore uniform coming to and going from parade, and we carried Carbine Rifles - dummies of course. Parade was at Sellincourt Road School, once a week during the winter: Band Practice was at Franciscan Road School and Sunday morning Bible Class, at 10.00am sharp, was in the old tin building , which few will remember. Seats were in rows, one for each squad, with the NCO at one end. Officers sat at the front and singing was from the BB hymnal.

"Going back to band - Mr Adair, from the Scots Guards Band, taught drummers and buglers and one can see him now, all 6ft 2in of him, marching up and down the hall encouraging us. Mr Stockwell taught us First Aid, using his son Robert as a patient. From the start the 70th had camped at Goring-by-Sea, with the 37th, and was able to do so again in 1914, just before war broke out. During wartime we thoroughly enjoyed ourselves doing 'exercises' with the local defence force. We would go to Tooting Bec Common, climb trees and keep our eyes open on the supposed invading army.

"Camping was 'off' during the war, but in 1919 we went to Lee-on-Solent. Camps at Stubbington followed. All were run very effi-ciently and one remembers most the last night in Camp, made memorable by Captain John Godfrey of the 37th playing 'the bells', as darkness fell. As a boy, securely rolled in blankets, you would see a group of officers gather by the Flagstaff, some holding an ancient sheet of music. Others shone torches while John swung his concertina to give us one of the greatest thrills of Camp.

Many senior boys were called up for war service and some never returned - one being our Chaplain, the Rev Albert Veryard, and another our Lieutenant, Clifford Blazdell.

"Mr William Cotsell was held in great respect. On parade or at Bible Class he was the Captain, but off-duty he was a great friend, helper, and advisor. He had a library of books, which he allowed us to borrow, and on Saturdays, after football, he would have small groups of us to tea. We sat on the floor listening to records on the gramophone and many of us got our first taste of good books and lovely music from those evenings."

"In those days, if you wished to go anywhere you walked, or rode a bike, so many a Saturday found us away to Box Hill, Leith Hill, Ranmore Common, or Wimbledon Common and on to Richmond Park. On most occasions we finished up at Mrs Becketts's general store in Ewell, where in the yard was a bath of cold water for us to have a sluice before going in to tea. Everything was 'ad lib'. Watercress, bread, butter, jam, and cut cake - as much as you could eat, washed down by cups of tea, and all for nine pence old money! Then we would remount and cycle home. We thought nothing of marching for a battalion parade to Stockwell, Clapham or Balham and back to Longley Rd - and loved it, the Bugle Band led the way."

Fred also tells the story of how at one Camp, the junior staff went down to the bakers after lights out at 10.00pm to pick up the following day's supply of bread. Whilst waiting for the bread to bake the staff were singing hymns and songs on the village green accompanied by John Godfrey on the concertina until they were interrupted by the village policeman who advised them to stop as they were disturbing the local dignitary, Admiral Lord Fisher. However, the policeman was sent on his way by one of the larger staff who dwarfed the village PC and pretending to be a Sergeant said "don't worry, I've given them permission". The PC left fully convinced by this bluff. However, on the way back to the camp field the party ran into a herd of cows, and the subsequent commotion caused woke the camp, and the wrath of the CO far exceeded that of Lord Fisher!

Returning to Frank Hysom it is possible to see the close relationship that developed between "C.O" and the boys. "I can recall spending the day of the funeral of King Edward VII (1910) walking across Wimbledon Common all day finishing up at Manville Rd for a wash up and Rose's Lime juice and a biscuit. I shall never forget him"

Both Frank and Fred's accounts give an impression of a well run, tight and efficient organisation, staffed by caring volunteers. The emphasis on drill should be noted and the standard must have been good as an earlier Company history records how the boys used Martini-Henry Drill Purpose Carbines, and how one ex-member of the 70th, Harold Bird, was glad of this instruction when serving in the army during the First World War, although he had some difficulty persuading his RSM that he hadn't deserted from another regiment when it was seen how efficiently he wielded his rifle

Camp in particular seems to have been efficiently run, and it is worth while remembering that in the early twentieth century that ten days away from home both for boys and for many of the staff would have been a novelty and a great treat, particularly as the majority of the working population were not entitled to and would not have received any paid leave .

The importance of camp to the Brigade, particularly in London at the time, is shown by the fact there was a London wide fund raising effort and boys were subsidised to the tune of two shillings a head in 1909 by the district alone, the equivalent of £9 a head in 2007. Some of the camp photographs of that era show many of the activities that were part of camp then, which remained a fixture: tent inspection, camp sports, devotions, swimming parade, tuck shop etc. These pictures also show that while the basic BB uniform of pillbox hat, haversack and belt changed very little during these years, indeed up until the 1960's, it was worn over very different clothing. Most boys wore very stout boots during the early years, and early Camp pictures reveal leggings and occasional gaiters. The uniform haversacks were a practical design, and would unfold to contain one's lunch on a Richmond Park expedition.

Throughout the first ten years of its life the Company strength averaged in the low 30's in number with a high of 42 in 1914 and a low of 27 in 1918. Despite the officer staffing difficulties at the end of war in November 1918 ,the Company was in a good position to move forward.

The Twenties and Thirties. (1919-1938)

At the end of the First World War additional staffing had been obtained from within the church with Percy Alderman, Stanley Clarke and George Alderman being enrolled as Officers. This under the continuing captaincy of William Cotsell (C.O.) provided a stable staff base for the next two decades.

The years immediately after the war saw an increase in Company strength with 50 being achieved in 1920 and an average strength of just fewer than 40. The company also started gym as a regular activity under Stanley Clarke's instruction using the old iron chapel building which was now starting to show its age and it's a wonder how the floorboards stood up to the activities of the boys. It is extremely doubtful as to whether the conditions would have stood up to a 21st century risk assessment and health and safety inspection! There were also safety concerns over the piano in the hall which Stanley Clark played whilst instructing, and these concerns were referred more than once by CO to the deacons to be met by the report that the piano was safe if used with reasonable care!

The Company Colours were presented at an unknown date after the end of the war and bear the names of those officers and ex boys who died in the forces. Their names are as follows "C. A. Blazdell, Harry Brickell, John Fletcher, Neil McLaren, Rev. Albert T. Veryard, Robert Walker and William Walker".

The Colours are still in use today and are believed to be the oldest Colours still in use in the London District, the crest still being the original BB crest without the red cross that was added after the union of the BB with the Boys' Life Brigade (BLB) in 1926. The latter act led to the discontinuation of the use of dummy rifles on drill parade and the commencement of a long local rivalry as the BLB company based at the Congregational Church in Rookstone Rd became the 28th London BB Company.

1918/19 also saw the unofficial start of the Boy Reserves, the under 12's section of the BB, which was started nationally in 1917. We know that the Boy Reserves existed as part of the 70th but they were never registered at HQ and continued to use the old title after it was changed nationally to the Life Boys in 1926. One of the members who joined on the first night of the Boy Reserves meeting was Alan Wakeford who joined as a 10 year old and served through the ranks eventually leaving as an officer in 1938. Percy Sore, who joined the Boy Reserves in 1929, gives a picture of life in the section at that time. "I joined the Boy Reserves somewhat reluctantly as a nine year old, being brought down by my brother Alf who was a Sergeant in the Company but a helper with the Boy Reserves. Alan Wakeford was the leader in charge - he was an easy going chap and wonderful fun. I felt at home on my first evening, it was lots of fun and laughter but not out of control, not obvious discipline but you could feel it there. A typical evening involved games, elementary drill and spiritual content - a happy evening that kept the boys coming week after week." The Boy Reserves had a stop/start existence through the 1930's, and was restarted as the Life Boys in 1938. Another member who joined in the 1920s was Jack Mayhew who wrote in 1998 "My remembrances of the 70th go back to when I was eight years old .I had under parent pressure tried the parish choir .So when a school friend introduced me in the tin hut to Alan Wakeford in charge of the 70th's Boy Reserves, and I found him to be a kindly man, I joined. It was great fun and I have been a member ever since. Vic Hopkins and Leslie Owens were my heroes and unknowingly pointed me in the right direction as too did Harold Barratt my squad Commander ,and George Alderman. CO Cotsell, the confirmed bachelor in his quiet unassuming way was the spearhead of all our varied endeavours."

After the war camp moved to Stubbington near Fareham on the south coast and the 70th continued to camp with the 37th. The inspecting officers camp reports from the 1920's give a picture of a well ordered and disciplined camp. The 1925 report for the 10 day camp at Stubbington is summed up as 'A high level has been attained. The discipline is good and of the right kind. The general tone is excellent. The general impression is that of a first class camp leaving nothing to be desired in any department and one worthy of the very best in BB traditions'.

High praise indeed. Other comments on the camp concerned what are described as the 'Commissariat and sanitary arrangements!' Water was pumped from a well supplied by a spring, which was passed as good. The quality of the food was described as the best and of the usual quantity. The latrines were screened, seated, pit earth covered twice a day. Refuse was also buried in a specially dug pit although swill was removed by the farmer for his pigs. Overall the cleanliness was excellent, leaving nothing to be desired. The cost to the boy for these 10 days was 30 shillings if at school or 35 shillings if working. This is equivalent to £60 or £70 in 2007's prices. Activities included organised camp sports such as football, cricket and rambles and a daily swimming parade with a fair walk to the sea.

Camp
Scenes
from the
1920's

Unlike later years there was no church parade on a Sunday but regular morning and evening prayers were held. This camp routine at Stubbington continued right up until 1938 with neatly laid out bell tents, a good selection of games including football of course, a camp sports day with its own specially produced programme and overhead flights by bi-planes from the nearby airfield. First time campers might have been surprised by the brailed up bell tents thinking that it was going to be cold at night without realizing that the tent walls came down. The Camp Vesper as sung then remained the same into the 21st century.

> **Great God who knowest all our need,**
> **bless thou our watch and guard our sleep.**
> **Forgive our sins of thought and deed**
> **and in Thy peace Thy servants keep.**
>
> **We thank Thee for the day that's done,**
> **We trust Thee for the days to be,**
> **Thy love we learn through Christ thy Son,**
> **O may we all His glory see.**

The spiritual side of camp was as important in the 1920's and 30's as it has been throughout the life of the company Jack Mayhew writes "I never missed Stubbington farm camp, when at an evening service I was converted. My commitment was cemented by the "concertina" hymns played by Capt. John Godfrey of the 37th, when we were tucked up in our blankets and bell tents. He could never know what message he transmitted by this means to us. Especially the last nights when swinging his concertina to play the bells."

Writing some seventy years later Vic Hopkins gives his own slant on a week at Camp. "Annually on the last Saturday of July throughout the 30s, wet or fine, the country town of Fareham in Hampshire shuddered under the double blow of drums and bugles when, band out front, the 70th and 37th London Companies of the B.B. marched briskly from the railway station at the start of a three mile trek southward to a camping site at Stubbington. Brazen echoes rebounded from buildings as buglers, cheeks distended, set a lively pace with a popular march supported by an enthusiastic rattle from the drummers which brought clusters of people to windows and street corners to stand and stare.

Clear of the town, the band continued to play as noisily but less briskly, as we marched at ease to an audience of placid-munching sheep which eyed us with indifference until a shrill blast from the buglers caused them to bolt and to huddle in protective corners of their grazing ground, bleating indignantly. The band rested, and the order given "March easy," we marched to the tap of a single drum and the cacophony of voices raised in a selection of then popular songs not to be confused with modern 'pop' numbers in the 'charts' - the lustiest or most rowdy being "blow the good old bugle, boys, and give a hearty cheer, step it out, the baggage cart is bringing up the rear; Send a wire to Cooky that we're coming down by train, Hungry and thirsty to Stubbington." which, if not the finest of lyrics, left no doubt in the minds of local inhabitants that we were on our way "to spend the happiest week in all the year." Singing ended, and marching at attention, we swung through the opened farm-gate to take over our canvas homes already erected in preparation for that week.

For my first experience of camp life when a lad in my mid-teens, rain fell steadily from early on Saturday morning until late on Monday afternoon, but, from the moment I emerged from the bell tent after a quick lunch in a large marquee, and paddled into a rain-soaked field to play volley-ball in bare feet --an unprecedented luxury hitherto--I took to the life wholeheartedly.

To-day, if I close my eyes and let the years flow over me, the Cookhouse chimney will still be sending forth its own brand of black smoke, and Cooky himself, bare arms flamboyantly tattooed, will be tipping into an urn of boiling water the day's ration of mutilated potatoes haphazardly scraped by the previous day's fatigue squad.

From a store-tent nearby emerge the rubicund figure of the quartermaster, John Godfrey, an undertaker by profession and a comedian at heart, wearing a boyish pair of khaki shorts, much faded by long service, and on his lips a boyish grin, unfaded although verging on a frown as he checks a list of supplies, anxious as always to ensure there is no shortage of food for the boys' meals. Alongside a hedge flanking the cookhouse the duty-officer for the day is squatting on an upturned bucket giving what help he can to his 'squad' with never popular 'spud-bashing' Work finished temporarily, he watches the boys scamper off in the direction of the tuck-shop for a fizzy drink or ice-cream, those glories of youth.

Boys tumble on the grass outside their tents in frenzied bouts of wrestling, while those less active lie in the sun or stroll across to C.O's tent for a chat. Away from the tents, a vigorous game of Puddocks (a cross between cricket and rounders) is in progress, fielders Scampering to all corners of a bumpy, grass-happy field in pursuit of a hefty blow from a formidable bat. As fancy takes, Reg Lane of the 37th quick of eye and strong of arm is the batsman and lone of the fieldsmen in the deep. Into a memory-blue sky soars the ball as if it has wings like a bird in flight and with religious zeal I keep my eyes on it stumbling through uncut grass, fearing to 'muff' so palpable a chance for even in a friendly game of Puddocks in a camp field, a dropped catch is a reflection of one's prowess in fielding.

Down comes the ball at last into cupped hands where providentially it remains to my relief or contrarily it slips through nervous fingers to the ground to my mortification. Still in the land of memory, a party of bathers filters through the gate leading onto a lane, costumes rolled into sun-dried towels, stepping out briskly for the shingle beach about two miles distant. My brow will probably be wrinkled with concern, not about safety, as C.O. is scrupulously thorough in his arrangements for bathing, but about how cold the water is likely to be; invariably, whatever the weather, I came out of the sea with face and hands a mauvish blue inviting some 'wag' or other to ask why I am wearing woad.

Light is beginning to fade now; 'Retreat' has long since been sounded and the flag lowered. A tail of boys shuffles into the marquee for supper, a grandiose name for a never-changing meal of three dry biscuits, a cube of cheese, and a mug of steaming hot cocoa. The smell of cheese, cocoa, and paraffin from the lamps remains with me till this day, indefinable, indicative of 'lights Out' soon to be Bounded at the close of a day spent in the open air with unlimited high spirits and shared laughter. Tightly cocooned within 'rough ~I male blankets' lying on a nightly-thinning straw mattress, a lumpy kit-bag for pillow, after a few moments of whispered chatter, slowly we drift into a deep, untroubled sleep. The notes of 'Reveille' sounded by a sleepy duty bugler waver on the morning air, rousing tousle-headed sleepers from dreams of representing England at football or cricket and summoning them out of snug pailliasses. Soon, heads peer through unlaced tent-flaps and ghost-like figures make their way across dew-laden grass to the latrines or the ablutions (enamel bowls on a wooden trestle). A flurry of soapy water over hands and face for a freshener and back we trail to the tent to make ready for Kit Inspection, camp's own brand of very mild torture guaranteed to ensure that everything in each bell-tent and around it is shipshape and Bristol fashion. Sgt. Roy Pitt a practised campaigner and a martinet at this particular pre breakfast exercise, confident as ever that his No.1 tent will take the award for the day with least deductions, checks that blankets are folded immaculately, brail tightly rolled and crease-free, kitbags squarely ranged, and all equipment correct, while we lesser mortals scramble around in an eternal 'flap' to be ready on time, dragging blankets into position and smoothing down the brail as best we can even as the C.O. is on the point of leaving his tent to start his rounds, keen-eyed, strict, but scrupulously fair. Replete with lumpy but tasty porridge, just occasionally singed --not burnt, quite -boys quickly demolish all traces of early morning kit inspection, and within five min~tes, each tent is upside down as blankets are tossed aside and kitbags rifled for some trifling article. Rivalry between tents is keen and standards of tidiness high but never is it allowed to spoil the harmony of camp life and the good humour among campers. Rigid and formal for a few minutes at the start of each day, we were as free, as energetic, as occupied, as wild as any present-day free-and easy' campers.

The wheezing notes of a concertina drift across the field from the marquee on wet days as John Godfery, eternally young, leads a session of community singing which is robust if not very musical.

All good things come to an end, B.B. camp being no exception. On the last morning, there is no time to be doleful. Bell-tents, our homes for a week, are struck, usually with efficiency but sometimes with complete lack of it which brings the tent toppling on top of the struggling 'demolition' team who are too busy laughing to care greatly. Off to the barn we trudge to empty flattened pailliasses (pally-asses to us) of their straw a task never as enjoyable as that of filling them on arrival. The last dishes are washed, cutlery greased, the site cleared of debris and we are ready to march out, leaving only one tent standing for a small rear-party and a row of lump-in-the-throat-brown circles to mark the scene of "the happiest week there is in all the year."

camp 1937

The company inspection and display was also a regular annual occurrence.Unfortunately we have no programmes from the period before 1938 but from the remnants of information available it would appear that the displays were traditional but not without their humorous moments even if they were accidental. Writing in 1958 about his first inspection in 1920 Ewart M Sutton wrote "When playing the side drum in the Band , after the rest of the band had stopped marching and playing , I continued marching (and playing) receiving a special "clap" from the audience . It was not amusing (to me at any rate!)". Also writing in 1958 G. Davison writing about the 1919 display said "At times I stuttered , at the display rehearsals I did well , but come the night of the display in a guard item I said 'Halt, who ,who, goes ,goes , goes there?'" . A third old boy from the same era W. Smith wrote at the same time " My most embarrassing moment was at an annual inspection. I was in charge of the stretcher party and we had just bandaged up a fractured leg and put the patient on the stretcher and I was given the order to move away when I noticed the inspecting officers eye staring at something on the floor , to my horror it was a splint that ought to have been put on the leg. Wasn't my face red!"

An innovation in the 1920's was the introduction of BB week, where boys collected money for Company funds. The first BB week in 1921-22 saw £5-15s-2d raised (over £200 at 2007 prices). This source of funding dropped during the 1920's to £4-3s-6d in 1928. This decline reflected the deflationary circumstances of the 1920's rather than any drop in giving or decline in collecting. Prior to the introduction of BB week the Company was heavily reliant upon subscriptions and the support of the church, as the January 1921 deacons meeting minutes record, when after an appeal by the Company all of the deacon's and the Pastor agreed to give an annual subscription to the work of the Company and the Pastor (Rev Fred King) also undertook to make an appeal from the pulpit to the congregation.

The merger of the BB with the BLB saw the 70th as a member of a much larger battalion. The Company was part of the South London Battalion which had the river Thames at the North and covered present day Wandsworth, Lambeth, Southwark, Lewisham and part of

Greenwich.

Upon this merger in 1926 the battalion strength went up to 78 Companies with 2747 boys compared to only 31 Companies in 1924 with 1589 boys. This increased number of Companies, particularly the number of local Companies, meant that there was less travel for football on a Saturday with the Battalion being split into regional groups. We have no complete record of how well the Company performed at football or any other competition during this period. However, Jack Mayhew who was a boy in the Company between 1928 and 1934 ,after service in the boy reserves ,recalls that the company always did well in the drill and first aid competitions and was normally in the top four of the football league with games being played on Tooting , Clapham and Wandsworth Commons and Garratt Green.

During the 1920's and 30's the mainstay meetings of the company continued to be Drill Parade held at Sellincourt School at 8.15 pm on Wednesdays and Bible Class at 10.00 am on Sundays, held in the Church Parlour for many years. Bible Class had a keen Missionary interest. The story is told of an occasion when C.O. was reading a Missionary story about the South Sea Islands. One of the squads in the Company at the time was composed entirely of boys living in Pitcairn Road, and the phrase occurred in the story, 'The dirty Pitcairners', whereupon there was loud laughter, and the squad concerned laboured under that name for some time afterwards! In the 1930's, the Class was held in the old tin building, the squads being seated in a hollow square and the Missionary stories still 'favourite'. Punctuality at Bible Class was encouraged by the doors being locked when the roll was called at 10 o'clock , and then being opened again after the roll had been called so the latecomers made their way into the tin building to sit in their squads.

The company however was not averse to using the new technology of the day in its activities, as in 1924 the church gave permission to fit a wireless apparatus in the lecture hall for demonstration purposes.

The arrangement for Company meetings being split between the old iron Chapel, Church and Sellincourt Rd School changed in the late 1930's with the development of the Sunday School halls ain Longley Rd and the sale of the old iron Chapel. All the youth work could now take place in one building which still exists today with the exception that the main hall as built was converted to the church sanctuary in 1973.

Arthur Bowbeer remembers the opening of the new halls in February 1937 and a sketch performed by the boys and written by CO as follows "I took part in the opening day of the new Sunday school building (now the church and halls) when the 70th did a longish sketch poking gentle fun at the new rules for use of the halls. Whether or not the deacons were amused or not was not clear." Once the new halls were opened drill parade was moved to them from Sellincourt School , however this presented its own problems as drilling on them was "like marching on a drum" .This effect was created by the cavity under the floor boards rather than the conduited River Graveney which was buried under the halls.

Old iron Chapel scene of many company activities before **1937**

Percy Sore describes life in the company in the 1930's, and William Cotsell (C.O) in particular who by now would be in his fifties. "CO was a strong disciplinarian but never raised his voice, he only had to look at you, not a stern look, almost a hurt look, to make you feel knee high to a grass hopper. On one occasion the Company fell in at the start of parade evening at Sellincourt school. The company was in 4 ranks, with supernumeraries at the back and the recruits just in front. CO was giving the notices, one of the recruits started swearing and cursing. Bill Daniels tapped him on the shoulder telling him to be quiet as the officer was speaking. He was thumped in his stomach. CO looked up and said 'alright, Robinson, you know where the door is, I do not want to see you until you have learnt how to control your temper and your language'. The boy turned on his feet and walked out."

Percy shows CO to be a father figure to the boys, despite being a bachelor, and a cultured man, who was able to descend to the level of the boys without them knowing it. One incident involved a rough house with a dozen boys piled on top of him but he just shouted the word "Company" and the group dispersed and fell in.

Arthur Bowbeer, who joined the Company in 1936 gives his view of life in the Company in the 1930's. Arthur says "I was invited to come along by a school mate, Ted Stephens, who also invited 3 or 4 other boys from my class at Ensham School which made it easier to join, including Gordon Ferriman who also eventually became an Officer. There was a gang of us in Valnay Street - Eric Piddington, Vic Stevens, Ron Betts and David Osborne, all members of the Company."

Arthur's views on the Officers and activities also recorded that. "I found that the Officers were very good in that they meant what they said and their' yes' meant' yes'. The captain, Bill Cotsell, who had founded the company in 1908, was a very gentle man and had a wonderful smile. We used to stand before him on a Friday evening when we lined up at Sellincourt School (the present hall had not yet been built) where we used to parade and saluted him as we paid our penny subs. At various times he had appointed a number of Officers including George Alderman. I remember Stan Clarke, a Lieutenant, took us for PT and gym. Another was Alan Wakeford whom I surprised on the first night when I said 'no' to his invitation to come along to football the next day. Another officer was Leslie Owens who was at the London School of Printing and later became the Principal. I enjoyed everything, but especially the drill which they did well. They had a system of junior NCO's and Reg Roper was our squad commander. However I did not want to go to camp as I was used to going about on my own, in particular I used to go on a tram to Waterloo to see the trains. On reflection I can see that the BB was made for lads like me and it encouraged us to mix. I enjoyed Bible Class and considered it to be a clear expression of goodness. I was in the habit of going to Sunday school at the Parish Church and found that the BB Bible Class presented Christ in an interesting way. In addition, once a month the CO would tell us yarns about brave Christian men, which we greatly appreciated. At that time we did not have visiting speakers. What greatly impressed me were the Battalion Church Parades. There we were marching up Church Lane in Tooting and we had no band then. But as we approached Tooting Bec common we could hear a number of different bands making their way towards the parade ground. Then there was a great snake of 800 or so boys as we marched off to a church, occasionally to Longley Road. On our own monthly parades it was the custom for one of the boys to pump the organ on church parades. One of the lads Ron (Spanner) Manning was inclined to lark about. One morning we were all surprised to hear the accompaniment to the second verse of a hymn fade away and then to see Ron come out of the organ loft waving the handle and saying "it came orf in me 'and"!

As the company entered its thirtieth year however, significant changes were afoot in the Company staffing. CO was now sixty and about to retire from the Civil Service. He had notified his intent to the Church to retire from the Captaincy and the Deacon's meetings for late1937 and 1938 record the search for a new Captain and indeed a new staff, as none of the existing officers wished to take over from CO or remain under a new Captain. One can only speculate as to why the other staff didn't want to take over. One possible reason was work commitments of the current staff. Another possibility was church difficulties either over the use of premises or something else, as the church records for 1933 mention what the Deacons perceived at the time "as a lack of co-operation between the BB and the Church. However, despite the criticisms raised, nothing could be done about the matter". Whatever the reason, the church in 1938 raised a completely new staff to start the new session in September. We know that CO's departure was kept from the boys until the end of camp .

William Cotsell

The Company Founder at Farnham Station in 1938 on the Journey home from Camp.

After retirement CO moved from Sutton where he had been living to Worthing, close to the pre-1914 camp site at Goring, although the area was fast becoming built up. After retirement there was a presentation to the CO of fruit trees which he planted in the large rear garden of his new house. The sense of how time consuming the Company work had become is best described in a letter he wrote to Fred "Tot" Thomas in February 1939 when he writes of "relinquishing my job with the Company". He also describes the presentation and the fact that "it was a representative gathering and I appreciate it very much".   There is also a feeling that he was missing the Company when he writes "it is all a bit strange after city life and it will take me a long time to settle down to the routine of retirement." William Cotsell lived in Worthing until his death in February 1958 aged 81. The following obituary written by one of his officers, George Alderman, was printed in the church newsletter and is worth repeating here.

It is only proper that the Jubilee Year of the 70th London Company of The Boys' Brigade should be fittingly celebrated and that it will be appears certain from all that one hears. It is poignant, therefore, to record that one face will be sadly missed from the celebrations to take place later in the year, for the founder Captain of the Company, W.E.H.COTSELL, passed away on February 15th.   As one privileged to serve under him as a Lieutenant for ten years, I gladly pay the following tribute to his sterling character and winsome personality. He was a Civil Servant, a bachelor, and his life interest was the B.B. Through its organisation and constitution he channelled the gifts and abilities with which he was endowed, to the spiritual and moral advantage of hundreds of boys.   He had no time for showmanship: all that he did mattered because all he attempted was vital. Nothing less than the best and the highest was worthy of the cause he served, namely, the extension of Christ's Kingdom amongst boys. Punctuality at all times was essential to him and his work. I cannot remember a Bible Class starting a minute late: ten o'clock was ten o'clock, and "fall-in" for Parade was blown on the dot at Franciscan Road School Hall on drill evenings.
There must be hundreds of men living today who are the sort of men they are because they came under the gracious influence of 'W.E.H.C.' to whom they owe a debt they can never repay.

Camp at Stubbington in the 1930's

The Coming of War and The War (1938-1945)

The gathering together and selection of the new staff team for 1938 is best told in the words of the new Captain "Bert" Porter writing in 1988.

"Just 50 years ago I felt a strong compulsion to offer myself as Captain of the 70th, having heard that the Founder - Captain William Cotsell, and his three Officers were retiring. The Rev Andrew Wright answered me by taking from his desk a piece of paper on which my name, alongside three of my friends was already pencilled. This was rather amazing. I knew nothing of The Boys' Brigade or the heavy administration a Company entailed. Rolly Clark was in a similar position; Chris Nott had been in the 70th for only two years as a boy but, fortunately, Jack Mayhew was already an Officer in a nearby Company and willingly agreed to join us.

"In September 1938 we started the new session - 19 stalwart boys, of real quality, and a keen but woefully ignorant bunch of Officers, apart from Jack. We survived those first few months - but only just. In February 1939 I was confronted by six senior boys who had decided to leave the Company - they apparently regretted the loss of the high standard of staff-knowledge and efficiency, so typical of the 70th for so long. After a sleepless night I saw the six again and persuaded them to have patience with us. We were learners, but meant well. As the staff improved in ability, so the Company increased to a healthy 30 in number".

Bert's account is backed up by the deacons' minutes that record the appointment of the new staff group as described by Bert, with the addition of the formation for the first time of a new Life Boy group under Jack Mayhew's leadership supported by Bert Thomas and Tom Godfrey. The Church also supported the new company financially, telling the wider church family of the new arrangements in the September Messenger newsletter and asking members to subscribe to the BB funds.

The local newspaper was also contacted and a recruiting campaign is recorded in the following terms.

"AN OPPORTUNITY FOR TOOTING BOYS"

"What will winter evenings bring to most boys in Tooting this year? Cold hands and feet for the must go outs. Puzzles, games , hobbies, books or boredom for the stay at homes.

No sensible boys will endure these for six months when he knows that the solution to drab and monotonous winter evenings is to enrol in the ranks of the Boys' Brigade! Run by men trained and dedicated to the edification of boys , every conceivable interest and activity calculated to build up and expand a boy may be found in the company. Such as gymnasium, ambulance work, football, swimming , sports and company drill. Not to be forgotten too, is the time spent when the boy goes to camp , and then for ten days he lives under canvas and revels to his heart's delight in fresh air amongst a host of friends.

Each and every one of these activities is designed and carried out so that a boy is developed , physically , mentally and morally , and he receives a training in Christianity that in all will equip him to face life cleanly, fitly and with his chin up. In addition the training will give a boy a pride in his Company and a personal responsibility through promotion in the ranks.

AT LONGLEY RD

During the next two weeks the 70th London Company are holding a recruiting campaign and every boy between the ages of 12 and 17 years is heartily invited to come along to the Sunday School buildings of the Longley Rd (Tooting) Baptist church on any Tuesday or Friday during these two weeks with a view to enrolment. It is a grand opportunity for any alert and enthusiastic boy.

THE LIFE BOYS

But boys under twelve years of age should not be envious. If they are between nine and twelve years they can join the Life Boys- and how they enjoy their evenings! Meeting every Wednesday at 6.30 pm in the same hall , they find Leaders just full of fascinating hobbies , games and Competitions which make the 90 minutes go like 19 minutes so you young'uns come along on Wednesday evenings and hear all about it.

Returning to Bert Porter's account he omits the fact that he was, at the same time, as taking over the Captaincy, getting married and his wife Avis says writing some seventy years later "On our honeymoon to Switzerland ,in order to ensure that his first drill parade went all right he took the drill book and officers manual with him."

Jack Mayhew's account is on a similar line "When I reached the age limit the 70th didn't need staff but the new 2nd St Helier did. This venture taught me a lot about boys and life, something that was to serve me in good stead. I was approached to rejoin the 70th in 1938 as part of a new officer team in charge of a group of boys well trained in BB tradition most knowing more than the officers about the BB. The new officer team were committed to the object and wanting to learn and serve they bought many talents and gifts to the task. The senior boys were a devoted group and were to prove to be the backbone of the company, especially for it's future when war caused the officers to be scattered afar.

At the same time as I returned to the 70th, I was asked to form a Life Boy team -now the Junior Section. Stanley Blake, Tom Godfrey, Marjorie Harding were enrolled as leaders. Ivy Clark initially as Pianist. With the assistance of Percy Sore, company members Billy Stiles and Leslie Wright we visited local schools and in a few weeks we had a membership of some twenty-five energetic boys."

At the end of Bert's first session the company again camped at Stubbington (and was duly doused with water as a new boy) and preparations were made for the new session with the new officer team better experienced and ready to go . However, the start of the second year under Bert Porter was rudely interrupted by an air raid siren just after 11.00am on Sunday September 3rd 1939, this marked the fact that Britain was now at War with Germany, This was shortly followed by the military requisitioning the church halls, leaving Bible Class as the only functioning Company activity.

Bert Porter continues the story "Threats of aerial bombing almost wiped out our weekly programme, leaving us with Sunday morning Bible Class. Then our Staff Sergeant, Percy Sore, cocked a snook at Hitler and pleaded for a Parade in uniform one Friday night, so in December 1939 we met in the Parlour of the old Church. What a tremendous thrill it, was as the Boys turned up and commenced to number ~ deep voices from the 17 year olds, 1, 2, 3, 4, 5 …becoming more high-pitched and more difficult to hear as the line went right down the corridor …22, 23, 24, 25, 26. No bombs came that winter. So we had weekly drill parades and even resumed first aid, P.T and parallel bars all in the Church Parlour".

The following press report of the 1940 Display gives a contemporary account of the early war period.

The 32nd annual display of the 70th London Company of the Boys' Brigade which is attached to the Tooting Junction Baptist Church took place last Friday. It was not only a very happy evening's entertainment enjoyed by a delighted audience of parents and friends but an object lesson in what can be achieved by cheerful perseverance , grit and co-operation between boys and officers in face of obstacles that might have furnished excuses for a temporary closing down.

The Captain's report graphically described these circumstances : "On Sunday September 3rd last, about 50 boys were expected to turn up for the morning Bible class held at 10 o'clock . By 10.30 only six boys and the speaker had arrived. They all went into the church instead , where the news of the declaration of war was heard. Nothing daunted , they carried on and by the end of October in spite of evacuation and other causes of depletion 20 boys were attending the class.

The large hall so essential for Brigade activities was occupied by the military and was not available until January 1940 .So the church Parlour was requisitioned and games , physical drill and parallel bar exercises were carried out in the confined space."

The report goes onto to describe the display itself .

The Brigade paraded very smartly for the opening devotions led by the Chaplain Andrew Wright neither the inspecting officer or his deputy were able to be present , the inspection was omitted. The article then goes onto describe the display programme which included a drill item , followed by the final of the best drilled private competition, a cycling item entitled 'we go a wheeling', which involved a lighted candle race on bikes! The captain's report was interrupted and finished by the gym squad bursting in and starting their item involved which involved both gymnastics and a PE demonstration.

The 1940 display co-incided with the end of initial phoney war period which was followed by the blitz of the summer of 1940 and the evacuation of about 20 members of the Company outside of London. Contact was kept with many of them who were based in Chichester and Wingfield near Windsor both by letter and by visits, often by Percy Sore cycling to visit groups of company members. The reality of the war was also brought home by bomb damage both to the church and the halls, the company being asked to provide first aid marshals during church services.

Life Boys, now under the leadership of Mrs Ivy Clark, was moved to a Saturday afternoon to avoid the black-out and in addition there was the gradual call up of the staff, and then later Staff Sergeants, to undertake either service in the forces or essential war work. Despite the war and the call up of the male life boy leaders the work amongst the younger boys was continued as Mrs Clark wrote in 1941 " The team has been left in the charge of Miss Harding and myself…A happy time was spent last summer at the Life Boy sports in June our team , came third. At the trek in July on Wimbledon Common , we were fortunate in wining the prize for the treasure hunt .Many evenings were spent on Figges Marsh playing games. Then came -"evacuation"- twenty four of our boys left us…Although we have a small team at present, the spirit and enthusiasm of these boys is most encouraging , and we are grateful to the parents who have sent them along so regularly."

With the other staff being called up and Lt. Rolly Clark being engaged six and seven days a week on war damage repairs, the Company struggled through the early years of the war. In the 1941 Annual Report, Lt. Clark reported.

"Since the last report we have had a serious drop in numbers owing to the evacuation of junior boys and war work for the senior boys , our present numbers being 12 boys and 3 N.C.O's . In spite of this , owing to a wonderful effort by Boys in BB week we collected £11.2.10 , 2/10d higher than last year". The report then goes onto report how "Last September it was decided that the N.C.O's should run the Company under the supervision of Officers in case the company should be left without staff We can see God's guiding hand in this decision as the company's activities you witness this evening are entirely the work of the N.C.O.'s and boys" Lt Clark then goes on to mention "the untiring energy of Staff Sergeant Percy Sore, Sergeants Bowbeer and Ferriman cannot be estimated ". The report also speaks in glowing terms of Mr. (Daddy) Nicholls ,who took over the boys' Bible Class during those anxious months and was to continue in that capacity for some years. Despite the difficult times the plans for the summer session were set out " We hope to keep alive the boys' interest during the summer months by such activities as cycling and swimming and cricket etc" Although the absence of a camp in 1941 was again regretted. The report finished with a word to the attendant parents "all these are doing their work nobly. Now do yours by sending your boys regularly."

Company Display 1941.

A press report of the display reads as follows

MODEL AIRCRAFT EXHIBITION

Clever Work of Tooting Boys

Boys of the 70th London company of the Boys' Brigade and life boys attached to the Tooting Junction Baptist Church are very air minded.

At their annual combined display and inspection held in the new Sunday school building, Longley road, on Saturday , they presented an impressive exhibition of model aircraft . The planes were beautifully made and the youthful designers must have acquired a great deal of technical knowledge.

During the evening the Company and Life Boys'team were inspected by Lieut. Stanley Clarke late of the Company who congratulated them on their smartness and efficiency. The chaplain Rev. Andrew Wright also praised their efforts.

Drill ,games , handball, skipping, gymnastics and figure marching were a few of the items given . A sing song was also very much enjoyed.

Arthur Bowbeer, Percy Sore and Ken Marsh with model planes.

Avis Rance nee Clark recalls one incident during the war involving her parents "During the War, Ivy and her husband Rolly were anxious to continue as far as possible with all BB activities. This was a difficult time for boys, with many families disrupted with dads away, air raids, food-rationing etc.

One evening after gym where Ivy played the piano to accompany the exercises, she and one of the boys had to walk home to Hawkes Road in the blackout. In order to get home quickly they decided to take a short cut though the local park that was closed for the night.

This meant the boy helping Ivy over a fence and eventually scrambling out through a hole in the fence on the other side of the park. As they were coming through the hole they were met by the patrolling Air Raid Warden. He was not pleased to see them out at such times and they got told off. They eventually got home safely to their homes!"

Company 1940

During 1941 Mr. Will Webb, a Police Officer, joined the Company as Band and First Aid Instructor, being promoted in the next year to Lieutenant and serving as Acting Captain until the return of the original officers in 1946. Normal activities continued, with look-outs being posted during air raids and the boys doubling down to the boiler room when things became too heavy. With the return of some evacuated members of the Company numbers started to increase again . The responsibilities that the NCO's took on board are noted in the NCO's minutes from July 1940 where they have taken responsibility for drill alternating between two of the Sergeants Gordon Ferriman and Reg Worby ; whilst boys also took responsibility , for the football team , gym and subs. The enthusi-asm of those senior boys was indeed untiring and the continuation of the Company over that period was in no small part due to their efforts.

As the war went on the Company gradually got back to a degree of normality with the church halls being used again and Band practice being on a Wednesday, Gym and P.T. Tuesday, and Drill on Fridays. The company at one stage went down to nine boys, but then out of the blue went up to almost 20. Ron Webb describes how the compa-ny recruited "We toured the locality giving gym displays , often on bomb sites. We transported the horse, springboard and parallel bars etc on a hand cart."

The use of the halls did cause some friction with the church as there was more than one note of damage caused by the youth organisa-tions. However, that being said there are other occasions when the deacons record their thanks to Mr. Webb for the work undertaken.

The Band grew, fifes again entered the 70th Band in 1943 and one of Lt. Webb's police colleagues, Mr. Ede, instructed the boys play-ing this instrument. Mr. Webb purchased some bugles from lads he saw with them in the streets and the 'Ship Halfpenny Fund' was started. The first purchase made with this Fund was a side drum for Solo Drummer, first used by Peter Knights. The band's early reper-toire included "Georgia , Onward Christian Soldiers and Light of foot."

The band's first entry into the South London Band Competition was in 1944 playing "Valentine" , coming a creditable 5th to the winners the 92nd who went on that year to win the All London Band Competition (Devonshire Cup).The final of which took place in the London Display at the Royal Albert Hall, the programme for which included a physical recreation item involving boys from a number of local companies including representatives of the 70th. This was the first recorded appearance by members of the company at this event. The use of fifes with the bugles was discontinued after 1945.

Ron Webb - Will Webb's son was the bass drummer in the band and comments. "The Company band was reinstated about 1943 at the instigation of "Pop" Webb as he was generally referred to . The band began as Drum, fife and buglers . Most buglers played both instruments. On our final approach to the church we often played "onward Christian Soldiers". Another favourite was "Georgia" which included the well known bugle introduction followed by the melody played by fifes."

"When the band was restarted the old bass drum was brought down from the loft above the present sanctuary , skinless and dirty. New drum heads were added and I used to take it home for cleaning , polishing and retensioning, on my bike three miles away. The history of that drum (apart from its size and weight) was that it was built prior to 1926 with the old anchor badge before the red cross was added to it. Later a goat skin was added to the bass drummers apron which on hot days was very unsociable, particularly for the solo drummer on one side and the cymbalist on the other side of me."

The band wasn't the only activity that the company was making progress with. In 1943 the 70th First Aid Team of four boys, Les Wright, Reg Lansdale, Len Stacey and Peter Knights, under the instruction of Mr. Plummer, a Police Officer, won the South London Battalion Shield. The same team also competed in the London finals that year which unfortunately clashed with a pre booked appearance in the 1st Farnham's display so after competing in the final held at the 6th London's HQ at Bayswater it was into a taxi to Waterloo and then by train to Farnham arriving just five minutes before the start of the display to perform an ambulance item.

Company activities in the 1940's

The Company also played its part in the wider war effort. During World War Two there was a new badge available, for "National Service." Harold Sporle and Les Wright, Ken Collins and Peter Knights are among those who won this badge. The first two for service in a canteen at Tooting Central Hall and for bicycle messenger work. This involved 100 hours of service. Many others laboured without a badge at waste-paper collection. This was a Saturday morning activity, fluctuating in popularity in phase with the price paid for the paper collected. At 8/- per hundredweight it was worth doing but not at 2/6! Many, many tons were collected, sacked and dispatched - right up till about 1948, when the demand fell off. Anyone who can remember those paper-bestrewn Saturday mornings will never forget them as long as they live. (How many thousands of comic papers had to be read before trading-in!) This source of income was very largely responsible for the purchase of further band instruments.

As in 1914, one casualty of hostilities was camp, with no camp being possible in 1940 or 1941. However, camp was held in rather miraculous circumstances in 1942, as Percy Sore recounts: "After a battalion officers meeting in early 1942 Phillip Rose, Captain of the 37th and myself both felt that we ought to restart camping. Mr Rose mentioned this to the parents of one of his boys, who knew the owner of an orchard."

Camp 1942 was held in an orchard at Chinnor in Oxfordshire with two rows of bell tents between the apple trees and a marquee at the head of the field. However the war presented other logistical difficulties as Percy continues: "We didn't have a camp cook. However, one morning on the tube going to work Phillip Rose was drawing up a camp menu, despite not having a cook. The man sitting next to him enquired of him what he was doing. Phillip explained what was happening and the fact he needed a cook. The man said ' I'm a London City Missioner, I'm experienced in cooking , I'll be your camp cook.' " Having worked out a menu and getting a camp cook there was then the added difficulty of getting food when everything was rationed. However, all the food needed for a full menu was provided and the camp was even able to enjoy the luxury of four ounces of chocolate a day, courtesy of the London Fire Brigade emergency stores. This was a real luxury as the sweet ration was twelve ounces every four weeks. As Percy says "every problem that came our way that year the Good Lord overcame". At that camp, the boys of the 70th and 37th were given the freedom of the fruit in the orchard and enjoyed swimming in the local waterworks! It was here that our very ingenious London City Missioner cook produced some 'almond flavoured custard' which was devoured eagerly. Not until afterwards did they learn it was actually burnt!

The Orchard camp 1942.

The following year some members of the 70th attended a Battalion camp at Eton. 1943 also saw a visit to London by 24 boys and the captain -E Provis, from the 1st Cowbridge Company in South Wales . The Welsh boys were accommodated with boys of the company and there stay coincided with the company display .One lad Pte. Kitkat sung "O for the wings of a Dove during the display and Captain Provis sung "Cwm Rhondda" in both English and Welsh during the parade service the following morning. The display also featured a guest item from the 1st Farnham ,which had been formed by Jack Mayhew the year before.

The difficulties of the war did not prevent the 70th from recruiting boys during those years. Two members who joined during the early part of the war were Peter Knights and Leslie Wright.

Les Wright joined the company in 1939 at the age of 13, having become disenchanted with the Scouts as they did nothing but play games. However when Les came in September 1939 he found the army in the halls and the Company meeting in the church Parlour. Peter Knights joined the company in 1941 aged 14, having moved into the area from Norwood. Peter joined he says "in a weak moment, being tempted by a regular game of football." He agreed to join thinking he would be able to get out of Bible Class. However, the informality of the class and the openness of it attracted him to stay, which he did, military service and studying permitting, for the next 39 years! Football was an important part of company life during the war and Peter continues in saying "Then of course there was the weekly football matches on Tooting Bec Common, the matches against the 88th, were always special .To think we actually played against Jimmy Hill." Despite the war the Best Drilled Private medal was keenly fought over at the annual display.   Les Wright tells the story of how when he joined the Company Ted Stephens won the medal and Les thought 'once he becomes an NCO I'll win it', which he promptly did beating Jackie Lemon, only to pass the medal on to Peter in 1942, which was presented, to Peter by Douglas Pearson Smith, the younger son of the founder of the Boys' Brigade-Sir William Alexander Smith.

The weekly programme during the war was: Monday - First aid: Tuesday - PT, box , mats and bars: Wednesday - Band: GLB met on Thursday - guarded by the Deacons from the boys, who still got through: Friday - Drill: Saturday - Football: Sunday - Bible Class. A full programme, despite the war and the fact that many boys were working from age 14.

As mentioned earlier, Will Webb, having been persuaded by his son Ron, had become an Officer and Acting Captain but he had little knowledge of drill. Instruction in this and PT was left to the older boys. PT was led by Peter Knights and Les Wright took the drill. As usual in 1943 they entered the Barnsley Colour competition an event never previously won by the 70th. The competition was based on Attendance, Drill and PT. The competition took place at the Welham Rd HQ of the 99th London. Will Webb marched the boys on and then handed over to Les Wright and the Company doing two section platoon drill came 2nd in the Drill , won the PT (old style set exercises to music) and won the competition, overall a very proud event. Shortly after this a doodlebug landed in Renmuir Street causing much damage to the area. Peter and Les both came from their houses with the aim of ensuring that the hard won Barnsley Colours were secure together with the other Company trophies. The blast had blown in the doors at the front of the halls but both Colours and trophies were rescued. The company's handing over of the colours in 1945 to the next year's winners the 47th was equally memorable as the colour party , which included Peter Knights , had to turn from Colour party to first aid team as they had to deal with five broken ribs on a 47th boy after a bad fall during a pyramid item. Fortunately this was an incident that the boys could deal with as they had been first aid champions of the South London battalion that year winning the Osborne challenge shield.

The Company took part in various parades, including dig for victory, as well as the normal twice yearly battalion Church Parades which were a tremendous sight. Companies followed their bands to the parade ground normally on Clapham, Tooting or Wandsworth Common, marching to the parade, then on to the church, returning to the parade ground to be dismissed, and back to the church - all on foot with more than a few miles being covered at every parade.

Sometimes the parades were to our own church in Longley Rd often with additional danger from the enemy as Ron Webb comments "Following a battalion church parade to Longley Rd we were returning to Tooting Bec Common for dismissal via Rectory Lane when the air raid siren sounded . The band was about 100 strong and we were going at it hammer and tongs. The officer in charge blew his whistle and we ceased playing whilst a doodle bug passed overhead. Following the all clear the whistle blew and we carried on as before."

Ron then goes on to say how sometimes enemy action didn't stop the basic company meeting's taking place. "On one occasion we arrived for Bible Class on a Sunday morning and found that all the windows had been blown in by a land mine the night before. We were issued with brooms to sweep the glass before worship began. It was somewhat draughty."

Les Wright is the first known member of the company to get the King's Badge including his 100 hours national service, and also the company member who attended the 1943 Diamond jubilee Windsor Castle Parade. This Parade has gone down in BB folklore , the boys gathered at Waterloo station and were transported to Windsor without knowing the purpose for their trip. Upon reaching Windsor they were marched up to the Castle where the difference in drill style between the BB and the army caused some comment from the Sergeants who escorted the BB group particularly the practice of looking in whilst wheeling. During the inspection King George VI who inspected the parade made his famous speech in which he spoke on how well the BB founder William Smith had built the organisation on the "twin pillars" of discipline and religion. Les however topped off the day with a return visit to the church halls in Tooting for the GLB display.

After the War (1945-55)

The end of the Second World War in 1945 did not see an immediate return to pre war normality as most of the staff were still in the services and senior boys were eligible for National Service. However, during the war Bert "Skip" Porter had kept in contact with both the pre war staff and the senior NCOs (who had effectively run the company in the early part of the war), enquiring of their well being and making sure that they were available to assist the Company after the end of hostilities. This was by no means an easy task as the men concerned were serving almost in all four corners of the world. However, 1945 saw Mr. Porter's release from the Air Force and his return to a Company of Boys who did not know him. Gradually the plans Skip had thought out during his war service were put into effect.

The Staff settled down as follows: Lts. Clark, Webb, Nott, Godfrey (also a Life Boy Leader), Sore, Bowbeer and Ferriman. Strength increased so as to justify this large Staff. Will Webb retired in 1946, after carrying out to the full his original intention of "having a worthwhile Company to hand over to the Officers upon their return". He served the Brigade after his Company service as Band Convener of the S.W. London Battalion for a number of years. One officer from the pre war staff, who did not return to the 70th, was Jack Mayhew who moved to Farnham in 1942. The company was so well served with officers that on return from National Service one potential officer - Les Wright was moved out to another company in the St.Helier area, whilst a future captain, Peter Knights, was held as a Warrant Officer for three years until a vacancy occurred. During 1947/48 Percy Sore was appointed acting captain whilst "skip" Porter completed teacher training classes. Skip returned in January 1949.

On the 5th May 1946 a memorial service was held for the four members of the company who lost their lives during the war. The four names (D.Coole, E.Gibbs, R.Worby and E.Morris) were inscribed on the company Colours in a matching panel to those who gave their lives in the first war. Their names are also on the Battalion War Memorial, which is now in the care of the Wandsworth Museum service.

From the evidence of minutes of the Officer's meetings it can be seen that the work of the company was meticulously and painstakingly planned. The officers met regularly for meetings often lasting until after midnight. A typical winter session would be as follows:

Sunday	Bible Class
Tuesday	PT and Gym
Wednesday	Badge work such as First Aid followed by Band
Friday	Drill Parade
Saturday	Football - often two teams.

These company activity meetings were generally held in the church halls with band at Franciscan Rd School and home football matches on Figges Marsh.

Each officer had responsibility for one or more areas of work. The Life Boys was run largely as a separate organisation and met on Wednesdays. It is also interesting to note the carrot and stick approach to Bible class with the minutes regarding football of "any member of the football team absent from Bible Class on the preceding Sunday Morning will not play" and a further minute stating that "the doors shall be continued to be closed at the end of the roll being called at the beginning of Bible class, to stop lateness."

The NCO's, that is senior boys who held junior leadership responsibilities, were responsible for organising their own squad of boys, including visiting the boys who were absent and filling out absentee reports. These were then used to update the attendance register but also give an early warning system if any boy was either unwell or was losing interest in the Company. This system worked well in most cases although it is possible that some NCOs may have pursued absentees over vigorously as one parent withdrew his son from the company complaining that "The absentee visits are like something out of the Gestapo!"

The Summer was even busier with the following programme.

Sunday	Bible Class
Monday	Wayfaring followed by signalling
Tuesday	Arts and crafts and fireman's badge

Wednesday   Band
Thursday   Cricket practice
Friday Swimming, clubroom and campers badge
Saturday   Cricket

All of this was for the princely annual sum of 6s 6d if at school, 13s if at work and the staff paid £1.7s 6d for the privilege of running the Company. The comparative figures in 2007 would be (£8.15; £16.30 and £34.50). Whichever way you look at it a bargain!

The minutes of the Officers meeting's also provide an insight into post war Britain where it is often forgotten today that rationing and National Service continued for many years after 1945. In them we find reference in 1949 to the officers giving up part of their sweet ration so that boys could have sweets as a gift for the Christmas Party. There were a steady stream of senior boys leaving the Company to do their two years National Service.

Display 1947

In the late 1940's there were a number of regular annual events in addition to the weekly programme. These included the battalion competitions, exchange trips with 1st Farnham, the Company Display, Christmas party and camp. This mix of group events and badge work meant that there was a balance between the needs of the individual and the establishment of a company spirit as the boys worked together for a common aim. There was also regular feedback to the Officers from the senior boys in the shape of the minutes of the NCO's meetings.

The ten years between 1945 and 1955 was a boom time for the BB in Tooting with, in addition to the 28th and 27th at the Congregational Church and Fairlight Mission, a new company the 192nd was started at St Nicholas's Parish Church. Despite this competition the 70th grew and reached "skip" Porter's aim of 70 boys for the 70th in 1952. This is in the context of the 70 boys being just the 12-17 age group. The main recruiting area was the area over the railway and on the roads off Figges Marsh with the Clark house at No. 1 Hawkes Rd almost acting as a second company HQ. Not all recruits joined the Company at an early age. Brian Rance, writing in 1998, said "As a very late joiner I had to suffer the indignities of recruit drill at the age of 16. But it was worth it to enjoy the many friendships and experiences of the two following years - especially as my brothers Gerald and Alan, also joined the Company and were members for many years".

The strength of the company was mirrored in the strength of the battalion of which it was a part in that the South West London battalion which covered the old boroughs of Battersea and Wandsworth was numerically the strongest in London, both at Company and Life Boy level, a position it was to retain until the late 1970's. Therefore to win a battalion event was some achievement and gave the winner, and only the winner, the opportunity to progress onto the London competition. The Company took part in the full range of battalion competitions with the occasional exception of gym. Travel to these competitions was normally by public transport sometimes with unusual consequences as Martin Nightingale comments "Stopping the train well outside Tooting Junction Station on the way to a drill competition because we were in line on the station with myself at the rear showing a red light , which the driver thought was a signal to stop. Not fully believing what he was seeing, because the light was moving about too much, he crept into the station shouting some choice words to the effect you stupid idiot!"

When Jack Mayhew moved to Farnham contact was kept up and the first exchange visit was in 1944 with a visit by the 70th to Farnham. After the war exchange visits were both ways and the closeness of the two companies included participation in each others displays and joint camps. Travel back and forth to Farnham was by train including full band equipment - Bass drum included. Accommodation was in boys families' homes. This arrangement continued well into the 1950's .

The Company display in the late 1940's was in what would be regarded at the time as a traditional format with items linked by bugle calls. In the years up to 1950 buglers were borrowed from neighbouring companies such as the 37th ,47th , 28th and 27th. The display would depict the normal activities of the Company, including drill, band, PT, First Aid and camp and would be on both a Friday and Saturday night with both events being 200 seat sell outs!   In general terms the display presented a highlight ,which remained with the boys for many years after they had the left the company, as the following comments highlight.
Bill Pizzey writes "What sticks in my mind were the annual displays, and how proud I felt in front of my parents. In the games section, I always beat my brother John, we were always put in different teams.   When I got home mum would tell me off for not letting John win sometimes."   Keith Holbrook said "The Company displays are a strong memory. They were very good and a lot of planning and effort went into them"   Bob Sansome said "the displays just stick in your mind".

After the war camping was resumed but with a new camping partner the 3rd Mid Surrey from Cheam Baptist Church replacing the 37th London who used the same site but went in a different week. Camps up to 1950 were at Goring Hall, and Ferring near Worthing. The arrangements for camp were in many respects similar to those set up under William Cotsell. The timetable would be very familiar to those that camped with the company at almost anytime:

6.30 am	Reveille
7.30 am	Tent inspection
8.00 am	Breakfast
1.00 pm	Lunch
5.00 pm	Tea
8.30 pm	Supper
9.15 pm	Lights out

Tent inspection was, weather permitting, outside the tents and there were regular morning and evening prayers with the option of Bible readings as well. Travel down and back was the same for boys and kit - the back of a lorry. No worries about health and safety or seat belts back then, and there was a guest day when parents could visit. Latrines were hand dug by pick-axe with sometimes painful consequences as Owen Clark found out with almost skull splitting consequences.

Owen's brother Peter gives his view on the camps after the war "As I recall it was often raining at the camp site on top of a big hill outside Dover (the site used after 1950) and half an hour's walk to the sea. The grass was long and you had to get up at 6.30 to wash in cold water in the rain. I am sure the weather could not have been so bad all the time. But earlier camps were at Ferring, near Worthing, in a field very close to the sea and the weather was better. We had bell tents, and at Ferring comprised about 200 boys with other companies in the battalion, as well as the company from Cheam Baptist church. Inspection was at 7.30 in the morning when we stood in a line outside our tent with the brailing rolled up and our bedding neatly folded before us. The conditions may seem a little harsh, but our Officers had just come back from fighting the war in appalling conditions, so to them camp was like Butlins."

Martin Nightingale who was a contemporary of Peter adds "we got up to the usual camp wheezes such one boy being sent by Sgt. Lee to ask Skip for a brailing spanner. The laugh was on Sgt. Lee as Bert Porter sent him back with an earth auger! My first camp I came home with a swollen knee, a black eye, and clothing in my kit bag covered in blackberry juice from a pie my mother had given to me for a midnight feast which never got eaten because those officers were snooping around too much! Good fun though. Townies at camp believing that some eggs found in a hay field were those of a wild bird. Arthur Bowbeer suggested that we take them to the cook (George, who gave up his holiday to cook for the camp every year) and that we could have them for breakfast. Wonderful things chickens!!"

In 1988 Bert Porter wrote that "Around 35-45 Boys attended joint Camps with the 37th and 3rd Mid-Surrey. The August Bank Holiday became a first with parents, so that we had up to 120 people coming in coaches and cars to spend Open Day with us in Camp. The Dads v Boys football match was a big feature of the day ... the Boys usually won, but I must confess that one year we had 16 Boys on the field, unnoticed by the Dads. Then a goal was scored and as the Boys lined up for the re-start the Dads realised how great were the odds against them".

Behind these accounts of camp there was however much hard work, particularly tying together the needs of the different companies and often liaising with other users of the site as the site would often be let to a four week syndicate who would pool various items of equipment. In addition considerable time was spent on the detail of the camp organisation including menu planning, activities and in particular the devotional periods. There was also the allocation of jobs and in particular the specialist jobs of cook and medical officer, which in some years there was difficulty in filling. Camp was in those days subsidised by the company and in 1950 the cost for a boy to come was between £2 (£48.80 in 2007 prices) and £2. 7s 6d (£57.95). Officers paid £3 (£73.20) a not inconsiderable sum of money when you also consider that they also gave up a week of what was in most cases a very limited amount of paid holiday from work.

The success or otherwise of one years camp was then fed into the planning for the next year. This included feedback from the senior boys and some of the issues from that period included whether senior boys should be allowed out after tea, evening rambles, smoking at camp, (from the reference it appears by officers as well as boys), and next years camp site. Many of these topics will seem familiar to those who camped some forty to fifty years later.

After 1945, the Life Boys continued to operate under the leadership of Mrs Ivy Clark producing a constant stream of boys for membership of the Company. The Boys came to join the Life Boys for a variety of reasons - Martin Nightingale who joined in 1947 writes "I was already attending Sunday School and couldn't wait for my 9th birthday so that I could be part of something that looked OK. I stayed because we had very good times mainly being involved in games. There was also some pride in wearing the uniform. The Leaders were people that we could look up to and who obviously enjoyed the fun that we all created. A bit of marching in intricate patterns was something new too."

Peter Clark who joined two years earlier wrote "As a 9 year old I went along with various mates from our council estate at 6 o'clock on a Tuesday evening. My mother Ivy Clark wore a three cornered hat in navy blue with a badge shaped like a life belt. She ran the team with various assistants, including Vera Bowbeer, John Ward and Elsie Goodson. There were about 20 or so lads, mostly in uniform comprising blue jumpers and sailor hats. We were inspected at the beginning of our meetings especially our hands and knees. After instruction and games the meetings usually concluded with a sing-song before the final prayer. Once a year we would go to Woodfield recreation ground on a Saturday afternoon for a battalion competition of potted sports, comprising such events as three legged races and throwing balls into buckets."

As well as providing activities for those below the age limit of the company proper, which at this time was 12, the Company Officers considered what provision could be made for those boys who reached the age limit of 17. There was considerable discussion but the Officers decided in April 1948 to agree to form an Old Boys Association.

The first meeting was held on Monday. 16th August, 1948, and Committee appointments were made as follows:-

President:	Chris Nott.
Secretary:	Peter Knights.
Treasurer:	Jack Lemon.
Members:	Ken Marsh, John Kensett.

A draft Constitution had previously been drawn up by Percy Sore, which was approved by the Company Staff. Item 2 in this

Constitution defined the Association's Object as:

"The advancement of Christ's Kingdom through and amongst Old Boys of the Company, the promotion of a suitable body of gentlemen willing to assist the Company and Church in any manner possible, and the provision of a Reserve of Officers for The Boys' Brigade."

The Association's programme included from the first, Bible Class and a Social evening. Monday evening saw Old Boys and ex-Officers of the 70th meeting together for badminton, billiards, table tennis. etc., while Bible Class was held on the first Sunday of each month. During the football season a team played in the Balham League and a cricket team in the summer.

In the early 1950s there were a number of changes within the Company. On the staffing side Peter Knights became a Lieutenant in 1951, Percy Sore left in 1952 and came back in 1955, and Chris Nott moved away in 1954. The staff were also supplemented with three further warrant officers in 1953: Alan Smith, Brian Rance and Owen Clark. However it was with the display that there was perhaps the greatest change. Mr. Porter came to a Staff meeting in June 1950 and presented the idea of "a theme running through the whole Display - something to connect up the items - avoid gaps - increase the entertainment value, and use those Boys who were otherwise difficult to fit into traditional items." The staff were somewhat taken aback when he continued to outline his first rough idea , which was to have finished up with some B.B. Boys being wrecked on a cannibal island, etc. etc.! This was turned down flat by the remainder of the staff, and something less radical substituted. The final idea which came to fruition in 1951 was "The BB on trial" where the suggestion was that the Clerk of the Court would introduce the items, thus cutting out the orderly buglers which had been "rather disappointing during the past two years". The following extract from the display programme gives more than a flavour of how the display was themed

" Public interest versus the Boys' Brigade…
The charge…
that the Boys' Brigade is based on a questionable foundation,
 seeks to achieve its object by methods

(a)   which are entirely out of date
(b)   which impose unreasonable strain upon its members
(c)   are at variance with modern psychology and
(d)   do away with the individuality of the boy.

THE HEARING WILL THEN TAKE PLACE

As Counsels for prosecution and defence call, examine and cross-examine witnesses, the Public should weigh the evidence submitted and judge for themselves…..

Are the aims of the B.B. old fashioned and unwanted? Or do they represent a solid basis on which a boy may build his life to advantage ?"

After being introduced display items would follow on to support the arguments made by the bewigged Counsel.

The general idea of a "theme" caught on and later displays were entitled "Willy joins the BB", " From BB to RAF" "Tour of London" - which included a Rolly Clark constructed front of a double decker bus from which the commentary was made and "The BB go a cruising". This last display included the idea of boys dressing up as "dusky South Sea Islanders" which took some convincing of the boys in the 1950's. It would be regarded as strictly NON PC now. The adoption of the themed display meant the presentation of badges and certificates was moved to a separate Parent's evening, although certain special company awards were presented on the display night. These awards included the Best Drilled Private medal, which was awarded to the private in the drill competition conducted in front of the audience on the night and decided by the inspecting officer .The Esprit de corps trophy which was voted on by all the boys and the mediated by the officers to see who had contributed most to the life of the company over the past session was also presented.

1951 was the year of the Festival of Britain and as part of the celebrations the Company took part in the massed band of BB bandsmen that marched past King George VI in Buckingham Palace, where the King received messages brought by BB runners from the four corners of the United Kingdom. The photographs of that day clearly show the band being led into Buckingham palace by the 70th's own drum major Brian Rance.

Owen Clark writing in 1958 recalls an incident whilst practising for

the Festival of Britain parade . " After one of the rehearsals for the Buckingham Palace Parade at Wellington Barracks a fellow from another company came up to me and said . 'there is a sergeant over there who wants to speak to you.' He pointed to the Sergeant's mess , so I made my way to where stood a burly sergeant major of a guards regiment. His opening gambit was 'what do you mean by making all this row outside my Mess?'. I was dumbstruck .Seeing my confusion , his face relaxed and he inquired 'How's Mr and Mrs. Clark?. He then went onto to ask how the 70th were progressing'. My bewilderment abated only when his face became familiar and I recognised him as Jack Warner who had passed through the Life boy team and been a member of the company."

The Band also played as part of the South West London Battalion item in the London District Display in the Royal Albert Hall , the

70th's first appearance in this prestigious event, where the guest of honour was the then Princess Elizabeth. The Company band was also in much demand locally, instructed by Peter Knights. They regularly led the Annual Church Parade of the Balham and District Boy Scouts, and also took part in the Mitcham May Queen Procession each year, often with the 92nd London. The Roberts Shield awarded to the winners of the Mitcham Band Contest was won in 1952 when it was secured in competition with the Mitcham Sea Cadets Band. (There has been no Competition since!). The following year the battalion competition was won for the first time, and also won in 1955. In 1954 the battalion bugle team competition was also won. Despite this success as a pure bugle band , it is interesting to note that as late as 1951 there were thoughts expressed at an officer's meeting of the band reverting to a drum and fife band ,which had last been seen in the Company during the Second World War. Peter Clark reflects on his time in the band during this period "In fact the band was quite good. It was instructed by Pete Knights, assisted by Mr Want and Ray Holder, an old boy of the company. We sometimes won the battalion band competition. On the same occasion there was also a bugle competition when we had to play a number of calls in unison. At the end of the competition the sound of the massed bands of the battalion playing all together in the school hall was deafening. I recall that there were a number of band members in our street who were supposed to practice with the windows shut. However sometimes there were calls that were answered up and down the road"

One interesting set of correspondence shows that the company's band work was not always appreciated by the neighbours even if it was just restricted to a few bugles calls on a Friday and the monthly Sunday Morning Church Parade. One resident complained to Wandsworth Council's health department who then visited the church there was a robust exchange of correspondence from Bert Porter enquiring how could four short bugle calls on a Friday night possibly disturb the peace and enquiring as to what sort of person was still in bed at 10.00 am on a Sunday morning. Nothing further seems to have come from this correspondence. Although matters could have progressed if the main band practice was held at the halls in Longley Rd , rather than Franciscan Rd school.

During this period the Company entered two football teams in the battalion league most seasons, these teams had mixed results

although the battalion second division was won in 1955. The availability of regular football was a recruiting plus and a sense of pride to the boys who were selected to play as John Ward writes "The key BB event for me was football. I first made the 2nd team because the captain, Dave Richardson, could find nobody else. I remember his doubtful look when I volunteered. Nevertheless, in the first game I played, I ran about Tooting Bec Common like a madman and kicked everything that moved, including occasionally the ball. I must have impressed somebody because I became a regular and then made the 1st XI. What pride when I first took home that yellow shirt with the Pegasus badge on the pocket."

In the early 1950's the battalion football rules required teams to turn up even if the Council had declared the pitch unfit and banned play, any team not turning up would forfeit the game. To the NCO's of the 70th this seemed a harsh rule and they persuaded the staff to lobby for a rule change. From Officers meeting this was passed on to the Battalion Council who agreed after a fair bit of debate to the rule change from January 1955, an example of lobbying working in the BB.

The Cricket XI were more successful than the football team, winning the Battalion league in 1950 and again in 1955. Not all the company's physical activities were as successful and the Officers meeting minutes note that in 1951 "the PT and gym squads require shooting."

Another popular activity in the early 1950's was the first aid class originally taught by a combination of Messrs Bowbeer, Nott and Brian Rance. First Aid became something of a 70th specialty, winning the battalion competition in 1953 beating ten other teams. The teaching of first aid was a definite example of lifelong learning as John Ward quotes "I joined the first aid class early in my BB career and was lucky to be placed in the charge of a new Warrant Officer, Brian Rance. Brian had the happy knack of combining enthusiasm with immense patience, and I stayed with First Aid until I left the Company.

I can still recite the mnemonics Brian taught us for the circulation of the blood and signs and symptoms of a fracture."

From 1949 the Company was also a regular competitor in the London District Cross Country. This event was held, at that time, on Epsom Downs and often had over 250 boys taking part with the first three competitors home counting towards the trophy. In this period the Company's star cross country runners were Owen and Peter Clark. Between 1949 and 1953 either one or the other of them were in the top twenty in London, and in 1953 Peter came 3rd overall. Owen's cross country abilities were still with him some forty years

later when in 1992, in his early sixties, he ran the camp cross country at Swanage and came first, although this may have been assisted
by the boys all being accidentally diverted to another finishing point!

Drill parade and Bible Class were to quote George VI "the twin pillars on which the Brigade was founded". Attendance at these meetings was compulsory throughout this period , and the other activities
were secondary to these. Drill parade would start with a formal
inspection in uniform ,which would have been polished and cleaned
beforehand and many a boy would have learnt the secret of how not
to get metal polish on a crisp white haversack, blancoing the thin
stripes on the pillbox and polishing both belt and shoes until they
were immaculate. There were mysteries as John Ward says "How
was it that the Inspecting Officer always knew that I had cleaned my
belt with disgusting "Duraglit" rather than beautiful "Bluebell" John
also goes on to talk about his experience of drill. "My wayward
limbs meant that drill was a particular trial and I was puzzled about
its objectives. However, for whatever purpose, I eventually learned
the subtle differences of 'standing at ease' and 'standing easy' and
'forming line' and 'forming squad'. I have no doubt that if the right
commands were barked today my legs would automatically move in
the right sequence for forming fours."

At both drill parade and Bible class the BB hymn book would have
been much in evidence and well used. Bible Class was taken by a
mix of the Company's own Officers and visiting speakers. The syllabus varied year by year, sometimes using the Brigade's own syllabus and at other times a separate syllabus derived by the staff.
Once a month Bible Class would be replaced by a Church Parade to
the morning service at the Church, and there were also the six-
monthly battalion parades, sometimes with 500+ boys on parade.

All of the above activities gave a fullness to the company programme of the time as Keith Holbrook explains "BB could take over
your life. There was something virtually every night with Bible
Class on Sunday , sport -football and cricket on a Saturday , there
wasn't much time for homework. One thing about being in the BB
when I was in it was that the BB was at its peak , not just the company but the battalion was very, very strong . I can remember the

battalion church parades hat were a very strong memory , we used to gather up on Tooting Bec common and the companies used to stretch right along the common along the football pitches (No Sunday football in the 1950's) a massed band a dozen companies or more , there were hundreds of boys , it was impressive to me it must have been a tremendous advert for the BB , the band made a marvellous sound. At that particular time there was very little else for young people to do . We had seven or eight officers here with different attributes that knitted together to form a very good and strong group of men to lead a company that was growing numerically year on year, one of the aims was 70 for the 70 which we actually achieved"

Company Band Marching to the Coronation parade 1953

The finances of the Company were largely dependent upon subscriptions, BB week and the display. Uniform of haversack, belt, hymnbook and handbook was officially priced at 12/1d but sold to the boys at 10/- (just under £10 at 2007 prices), and the sums raised at BB week, which were often over £100, were normally split between equipment (e.g. a set of football shirts costing £10 in 1952) and day to day running costs after the company had paid the sum required by BB HQ. In order that the boys could see the benefit of their labours, which involved enlisting voluntary contributions from church members, families, old boys and friends, the equipment purchased was placed on display for all to see once purchased.

After Christmas, in January each year, the Company supper was held and a familiar pattern emerges year after year. The 1953 supper gives a flavour for what one of these evenings involved.

Starting at 5.30 pm with a puzzle corner;

6.00 pm   the supper itself with turkey, chips and beans, being followed by cakes, jelly and ice cream.

6.45 pm   team games such as balloon bursting, pea picking up, and balloon and candle race.

7.45 pm   an item presented by the NCO's.

8.00 pm   A village fair in the main hall

8.45 pm   Films - these would include cartoons and short films by Abbott & Costello

9.45 pm   Vesper and Benediction

The Officers would serve the first course of meals and the NCO's the second course. It would appear that most years a good time was had by all.

From 1951 Camp moved to just outside Dover, the site was some distance from the sea as John Ward recalls "My first Camp was at Dover. We travelled down with our kitbags rattling around in the back of a furniture van. No sissy worries about seat belts and the like in those days. I believe that I had the princely sum of fifteen shillings pocket money to last me all week. My chief recollection of Dover is that you had to walk forever to reach the sea".   The distance to the town was also a problem for the NCOs who at one of their meetings in 1954 recorded the following about the 1953 camp "It was suggested that the Sunday Church parade did not involve a

Camp 1953

three mile march into Dover, arriving as a shoddy crowd in a motley array of clothes, perspiring and too tired to give complete attention to worship. As an alternative to this event it was suggested that the company might proceed to the church at Church Hougham for a service conducted by the staff." Skip Porter's response was as follows "your picturesque description of our parade arriving at Dover a little travel stained was not considered to be accurate in every detail. The distance is but 2½ miles each way, of which nearly one mile last year was travelled freestyle until we reached the road. The officers did not all agree that such a distance imposed to great a strain on boys of between 12 to 18. Your idea of holding the service at the village church was not thrown out and will be discussed at the next camp meeting"

The same meeting notes a request from the NCO's about "camp Lady friends". "It was requested (by the NCO's) that there might be no persecution or condemnation of the formation of friendships outside of the camp, as it tended to aggravate the complaint which thrives on persecution and will always find a way" Skip's response was as follows "Last year this point was mentioned by us at one camp meeting on a Friday evening - but never at camp. Secondly we do think lady friends can be left at home for one week. We do not anticipate any emphasis for this year and we trust that all NCO's will be satisfied and not feel driven into the feminine arms."   From the record we don't know how successful Skip was in his request to the NCO's but it is suspected that the 'no fraternisation with the local girls rule' was probably broken in 1954 as it was in many another year.

One of the primary purposes of Camp, from the Officers' perspective at least, was the chance for boys to hear the claims of Christ on their lives. The regular devotional periods in the morning and in the evening, opportunities to get involved in regular systematic Bible reading and tent prayers at night could all lead to an atmosphere where boys might consider the Christian Faith in a serious way. However, last night frolics and feasts were not always conducive to this and in one year at least there was much post camp discussion on how to deal with this issue.

The devotional periods would often be shared out amongst the staff, and the talks would often be based upon BB related activities such as bugle calls or drill related activities. A talk entitled "Halt and About Turn" would be about stop, think, and consider ways, conviction and conversion. "Keeping Step" would be about wrong ideas, difficulties and self discipline. But the purpose of the talks was about practical application of Christian principles.

After camp in 1955 the officers met to plan the new session and its worth repeating in full the minute in the officers meeting of the 8th September 1955 concerning the announcement of Skip Porter's retirement as company captain. "It is almost impossible to make adequate record here of the debt the company owe to his leadership. Some attempt should be made to record his untiring devotion to the work of the Brigade as a whole and to the 70th London Company in particular. For seventeen years, with some breaks due to the war and training courses, Mr. Porter captained the Company and built it up

Skip Porter's last parade night 1955

from a handful of boys to the second largest Company in the South West London Battalion. No man could have given more in time, talent, energies and Christian love for Boys than he did, and his retirement will be a great blow to many serving Boys, Old Boys and to the present Staff to whom he was always an inspiration and a 'brother'. With him will go the best wishes of all the Company and staff and a hope that we shall not be forgotten by him for it is sure that he will not be forgotten by us.   May God continue to bless him and his family as they join the fellowship of the Church at Morden."

Writing some thirty years later in 1988 Skip wrote the following about his abiding memory of his time as Captain.   "I have three abiding memories of those years in the 70th. The amazing reliability and devotion of all the Officers. The list of 25 current Boys passed on in 1955 as having all made a decision to serve Christ. The numerous other Boys to whom the B.B. had shown a world of higher standards."

Bert later served as honorary president of the Old boys association until he moved away from Morden in the late 1960's.

The late Fifties -1955-61

The Company in 1955 was of a good strength and well staffed, a fact that the new Captain Arthur Bowbeer acknowledges writing in 1988 - "I inherited something like 60, plus a strong Life Boy Team, six Lieutenants, Warrant Officers and Staff Sergeants - to say nothing of dedicated Instructors such as Mr. Want (Band) and Brian Rance (First Aid)." Arthur goes on to talk about the difficulties that large numbers brought. "Those large numbers created their own problems. It was less easy for the Captain to know all the Boys and the tendency was to 'run it by the book', so that fairness prevailed ... but our caring was sometimes on the harsh side. Imagine the feelings among the Boys when, on a Parade Sunday, the Company fell-in in the Hall (now the Church) and it was realised that the Band exceeded one-third of the Parade strength. Imagine too how the Band Officer, Mr. Flint, felt as he chose two from the Band to march with the Company and thus obey the rules in 'The Manual'. Hard, yes, but the two unfortunates always played after Church, while two others fumed at being 'dropped'."

Band was an activity that happened both summer and winter regardless of the instructor with Peter Knights and Mr. Want being

replaced by Brian Flint and Martin Nightingale. Martin was the drum instructor and recounts the following "As a drum instructor I tried to phone Brigade H Q to talk to the composer of the march Royal Albert Hall ,which had been set by a Dave Cherry who worked at HQ. A very polite voice answered the phone and said he did not recognise the name of Dave Cherry but would check to see if he did in fact work there. After a few minutes he came back to say that there was no Dave Cherry working there and asked the question, why did I want to talk to Dave Cherry. I explained that the march he had written needed some clarification. The man then asked where I thought I was phoning to which I replied Brigade HQ. He then very politely told me that he was the Archbishop of Canterbury and I had rung Lambeth Palace, not Brigade HQ, and wished me well for the competition ,which I think we won." However, it wasn't always plain sailing as Martin goes on to tell "I couldn't find our solo drum-mer Jackie Fishpool as we boarded the coach after the first of three performances at the Albert Hall. This was the Friday night and I had not been too happy as Jackie had jazzed up the drum solo. No mobile phones in those days so we set off to get the rest of the band back home. I went to see Mr. & Mrs. Fishpool to tell them that the police had been informed but when I got to their house they informed me that Jackie was already home and was unfortunately in a diabetic coma having not taken his insulin! A substitute was found for the other two performances and very good too!" (This was prob-ably the 1960 London Display when the Company took part in a band item with a number of other companies from the battalion). During this period the band had a good competition record, winning the battalion trophy four times in six years (1956,1958,1959 and 1961) a good record in what was still the strongest London battalion. In fact in 1959 the band came very close to competing in the Devonshire cup final (The all London Bugle Band competition) as this extract from the Captain's annual report confirms. "During the last few weeks we have won the Battalion Band competition , fought our way through the South London Competition and finally finished fourth in the all London Competition. We might have bettered that if for reasons of illness and work three of our band had not had to miss the final round. However the reserves who were brought in at the last minute did extremely well as the result shows"

The subject of discipline in the Company was raised quite often in the officers' meeting of the late 1950's both in terms of steadiness on drill parade but general conduct as well. The conclusion in 1956 was that "the Company was reasonably free from bad language which was prevalent in some other companies. The Company was not too bad in comparison with others but fell short of it's own high standards." In 1958, the subject was again discussed with particular regard to band practice but also to matters in general and again a decision was made to retain the rule that if a boy was not at Bible Class for any reason he couldn't play football on the Saturday, and this was now extended to cricket, although boys who were attending

a family holiday were exempt from the summer rules! The following year the officers' meeting minutes record that "it was agreed that a firm line would have to be taken in the ensuing session and that it would have to be 'obedience or out' and in connection with this it was agreed to send a letter to all company members, before the start of the Winter session, setting out the terms of service in the 70th, and it was further agreed that these should be communicated to the NCO's at a special meeting before the letter was generally circulated."   The letter must have had some effect as in the following session the company came a close 2nd in the Battalion Barnsley Colour competition the results of which were based on the drill competition and attendance at drill parade and Bible Class and this result was helped considerably by the fact that the Company had the best attendance record in the battalion. However, the subject was raised again in November 1960 this time by the NCO's who complained about "the practice of some boys to go for a smoke during club room and irreverence at Bible class". This time the Officers' response on smoking was "to agree to take the appropriate action to stop smoking but it was stressed, as always, that the NCO's should give the lead." One wonders if the NCO's themselves were sneaking out for a quick fag. With regard to Bible Class the Officers response was limited to the fact that hymns might be sung too fast whilst the vesper was a dirge!

Drill was a routine part of the BB in this time and Mike Wallace describes his early induction into the company "A Life Boy at Gorringe Park Senior School within our group of friends asked if we would like attend his going up into the Company so the next Friday I and two others went along but within a couple of week. I was the only one still attending from our group. Drill training for new boys was under Mr. Bateman [Fred] saluting simple marching etc. Once while standing in front of us recruits in the back hall Mr.B. did three large steps and the newest recruit left us as a mouse bit the dust. After six weeks we each joined one of the squads for inspections and were allowed to drill with the main company which for most of us was difficult as they were so tall and we were so short except Raymond Parker [Nan] who was already about 5 foot six tall."

The company activities continued on the same pattern as under Bert Porter with the winter programme of Bible Class and Drill continuing on Sundays at 10.00am and Fridays at 7.45pm respectively, Band on Mondays at Franciscan School and box work and gym on Wednesdays preceded by first aid. This regular routine was potentially disrupted when the church moved Sunday School from an afternoon to during the morning service, but there was no record of any discussion on Bible Class being moved to accommodate this move or of merger with the Sunday School the main issue being that the hall used for bible class , then the Junior hall , would have been used by both groups. With the BB starting at 10.00am and the Juniot Church at about 11.15am.

In common with virtually all BB companies in the 1950's the 70th used the Brigade Bible Class handbook, which was issued annually . The talks were led by a mix of officers , old boys , church members and occasionally visiting speakers. This gave the continuity of the lessons from the handbook but variety from a wide range of speakers , the range of speakers available was so wide that it was rare for an officer to speak twice in the same session. Every second Sunday in the month the routine of Bible Class was broken up by the monthly Church Parade where the company would meet in the halls before the 11.00am service and then parade around the local streets band playing. These were special occasions as Mike Wallace says "Monthly Church parades in my first year can never be forgotten try-ing to keep in step and watching Vincent Price throwing the mace and twisting it in the air was a real sight. Once a year there was the battalion church parade with so many boys and officers it seems dif-ficult to believe how it was organised so well"

Badge work was largely concentrated on the summer months. There were changes to the Company staff in this period with Peter Knights leaving for four years due to work and study commitments, and Percy Sore left for ill health. The staff was enhanced by Fred Bateman who was an ex Officer and boy of the 9th London. In 1960 Brian Flint left the staff on moving out of the district and Peter Knights returned.

As in earlier years much of the work in the winter session was tar-geted towards not only the boys being able to achieve their badges under the award system but also towards the various Battalion com-petitions. As has already been mentioned the Company Band was successful in the late 1950's and early 1960's but the success in First Aid was even greater - between 1958 and 1967 the Company had ten unbroken years as Battalion champions and in five of those years it was also London Champions, the Company's first ever London tro-phy.   In the early years first aid classes were led by Brian Rance. Arthur Bowbeer writing in 1988 comments "First Aid to the injured hardly exists as a Battalion competition today, but in the late '50s it was deadly serious. Mr. Rance and young Will Ward pioneered the use of mocked up injuries, some of which were so good and convincing that those who were unaccustomed to such games would turn quite pale". The First Aid team was so good that it even beat its own instructors as Peter Knights wrote back in 1968 "The local St. John's Novices contest, which we originally entered 'for experience' and won, was eventually denied us.   On one occasion our novices beat a team comprising their own Instructors."   In other years such as in 1962 the Company's overall standard was so high that the B team came 2nd in the Battalion, whilst the A team went on to win the London.

Brian Rance's technique for teaching first aid was effective. Speaking some 50 years later in 2007 John Ward recalls " I did first aid something that you wouldn't do at school .I remember they taught us a lot of mnemonics which I can still recall such as signs and symptoms of a fracture "Peter , left , shocking, dirty shoes under chair" which meant - pain, loss of power, shock, deformity, swelling ,unnatural mobility, crepitus and discolouration""

In the late 1950's one of the first London Competitions to be held each session was the London Cross Country. This event was entered by many London companies and to get a high position based on the three highest placed boys was some achievement. In the 1958 race the 70th were second and John Ward who was the first 70th boy home in that team, finishing 13th, wrote "Amongst my most vivid recollections as an athlete are of the London cross-country Championships on Epsom Downs with over 200 runners taking part."

In the summer athletic prowess moved to track and field again initially under the tutelage of Brian Rance.   The 70th had a record of achievement at the Battalion athletics, which mirrored that in first aid with 11 victories between 1957 and 1969. In some years the margin of victory was staggering as in 1958 when Arthur Bowbeer wrote; "In June (1958) we won the Battalion sports cup for the second year running - this time with a record number of points both for this Company and the Battalion, scoring 363 points - 159 points in front of the next company.   In all we won 13 of the individual events and all three relays and the boys came home with 25 medals between them."

Throughout this time the battalion athletics were held on two days with the heats on a weekday evening - often the Monday and then the finals on the Saturday. The Athletics covered three age ranges with the successful winners of each event normally then being selected for the battalion team to compete in the district competition. The Company's relative strength is shown by the fact that in seven of the eleven years that the 70th won the Battalion athletics, the Battalion then won the London event. The company were possibly helped by the judicious spending of some of the BB week money in 1957 on practice field event equipment (shot, javelin and discuss) as

well as six pairs of shorts and some running spikes - the latter being important on the cinder tracks of the time.

Throughout the late 1950's the Company had teams in both the over 15 (senior) and under 15 (junior leagues) ensuring regular football most Saturdays during the winter, often in conditions that would not have been allowable in the twenty first century. The Company had mixed results in the leagues over this period never quite being strong enough to win. However the Cricket league was different in that the 70th continued the winning way of 1950 with wins in the Cricket league in both 1957 and 1958. The ability for boys to play a variety of sport both summer and winter against other strong companies was no doubt an important part in keeping up company numbers and spirit during these years.

The arrangements for changing and playing were somewhat different to that of the 21st century as the following memory from Mike Wallace shows "Saturday afternoon was football. The juniors' pitch was at the Three Kings at Mitcham.We had to change behind a large oak tree and obtain the posts and cross bars from the rear of a Pub on the other side of the road. When in the Seniors our goalie Albert King did an unbelievable kick from our goal and it landed in the opposite goal. The ref. could not decide if it counted. On another occasion Albert and I were in our goal area. This was at Wandsworth Park pitch by the Thames the fog was so bad that day, we could not see the centre of the pitch and then out of the mist came the opposition's biggest player over six foot and built like a tank. Well one of us had to go forward, here my memory fails me , I know one of us was brave."

One new activity that started in the late 1950's was the Duke of Edinburgh's Award.   In part this was complementary to the Brigade's existing award scheme with links in the physical, educa

Ralph Price and Alan Rance at Buckingham Palace following receipt of their Gold Duke of Edinburgh's Award

tional and interests section, but there was a new element of expedition. At the bronze stage this was 15 miles, silver 30 miles and gold 50 miles, with the participants carrying everything required. In addition to the distance the terrain became progressively more difficult with the Gold expedition being in wild terrain such as Dartmoor. The 70th were one of the early enthusiasts for the award as this quote from Arthur Bowbeer's 1959 annual report states "Before we leave last summer (1958) I must tell you of the enthusiasts who worked like stink to gain their Duke of Edinburgh's award. We are proud to say that the 70th was the first Company in this Battalion to start on the Duke of Edinburgh's award scheme and the first successes were gained last autumn when four boys, having completed their tests in Public Service, Physical fitness and Hobbies as part of the BB Badge system, qualified for the bronze standard award. Two boys went on to take further tests , including a 48 hour expedition covering 30 miles on foot carrying full camp kit and finding their way only by map reading , and qualified for the silver award." The officer's meeting minutes record that the first ever Duke of Edinburgh's award - at Bronze Level -to a member of the 70th was Ron Sale.

The two silver award winners of 1959 Alan Rance and Ralph Price and in 1961 they received their awards at Buckingham Palace. The Instructor was, again, Brian Rance. Perhaps the most heroic act carried out during all the expedition training was the three day, 50 mile trek by Peter Ellis, who went only to make-up the number. He fell into quite a deep Dartmoor stream and as he was a non swimmer the only concern of the others was of course for the food-pack on his back!

1958, saw the Company reach its 50th anniversary. As part of the celebrations a re-union dinner was held on the 13th December. Every old boy whose address could be traced was contacted, and 52 sat down for a four course dinner. To quote Arthur Bowbeer "what reminiscences were heard that night - a feast of memories that gladdened the heart. Our old Boys came from near and far - some a 3d. bus ride, others at considerable expense, every man drawn by the bond that unites those who serve in the Brigade." Amongst those who attended was Frank Taylor one of the original Officers. The senior boys and NCOs of the Company who were uniformly dressed in grey trousers, white shirts, bow ties and dark jackets served the meal.

Throughout the period the winter and summer programmes were as regular as clockwork with something on most nights as Alan Rance recalls

"In the boyhood years of eleven to eighteen, the BB was everything to me. Every day of the week took up some kind of activity. This was of course before the age of television, computer games and specialist sports clubs.

Monday evening was band practice night at a local school. Drummers and buglers practised separately for the first part of the evening and then the whole band came together to try to sound something musical. At the time of the Battalion Band competitions, there was inevitably more keenness to practice and sound good.

Tuesday evening in the summer meant 'wayfaring' activities, leading to the Wayfarers Badge. We would work on simple woodworking projects or making straw baskets. There was the occasional country ramble to help spot wild flowers and trees.
In the winter there were First Aid classes. Here as a 'casualty' you could experience being splinted up, covered in bandages, carried off on a stretcher, and if you were unlucky being pulverised by an enthusiastic resuscitator

Wednesday evening in the winter this was Gym night. Essentially for the fitter boys who would leap around on a range of equipment including the 'parallel bars', 'box' and 'horse'. In the summer this evening became the 'athletics practise night' at the Tooting Bec Running Track. The many successes of the 70th's athletics team were the result of lots of hard practice on such nights.

Thursday evening This was generally a 'free' evening. However, the Girls Life Brigade met on this night, so there was always the possibility of some romantic liaisons with the girls afterwards!

Friday evening in the winter was the important and 'compulsory' night -- drill parade.Here we were expected to turn out with immaculate uniforms, all gleaming with the help of boot polish, 'meltonian' [whitener] and 'bluebell' [metal polish].After inspection there would be drill. In the summer, Friday night became the more relaxed club evening.

Saturday was sports day. Football in the winter, cricket in the summer.

Saturday evening was Youth Club and a key social event in the week at the Sunday School halls, with table tennis and jiving on offer. This was the essential place to be if you were to start a romance. Of course there were many dramas on such nights with couples breaking up or getting together.

Sunday's Bible class was the other 'compulsory' event in the week. Every month in the winter there would be a drill parade. This would involve the whole company, [up to 70 strong] being led by the bugle band on a march around the local streets. This would always be embarrassing when you marched down the road you lived! The band would return to the Church where we joined the Morning Service."

During the late 1950's the Old Boys Association continued to meet regularly on a Monday evening with Bible Class monthly on the first Sunday of the month. There continued to be a number of social events including a Ladies night, and Football and Cricket teams continued to play in local leagues the latter often with more success than the former. In addition the association would often provide an item for the display, normally gym based and provide assistance when required for various functions or activities.

In general with most of the time the Company has existed it has had good relations with the Church. In the mid to late 1950's this was no different, helped in part by the steady numbers of boys who were baptised and entered church membership. However, as is the way with these things there were sometimes causes for friction due in part to differences with other organisations within the Church.

This extract from a letter to the Company from the Church deacons in May 1956 gives some indication of the friction ,which could exist and also some idea of where the company stood in the "pecking" order of organisations. "At their meeting on Thursday last the deacons decided that room 4 in the Sunday school buildings should be reserved for the use of Christian Endeavour and YPF and that the room is to be kept locked. This decision follows regretfully the receipt of complaints regarding the state of the room and damage to C.E. equipment, etc. The question of blame for such damage etc., was not considered by the deacons but they feel most strongly that in view of the part CE seeks to play in the life of the church it should have a place which it can clearly and undisputedly regard as its own. This decision affects the BB in that it will be necessary for the Monday evening Ambulance class to meet elsewhere." It is interesting to note that the letter was kept on file and some five years later just before his retirement as Captain, Arthur Bowbeer noted on the letter "This appears to have been forgotten - thank goodness!" The comments by the diaconate show that the 70th's programme at that time was so extensive that special arrangements were needed to enable other organisations to have a place to use on the premises. The odd hiccup aside relations with the Church were good and the BB boys, Staff and Old Boys assisted with church maintenance including redecoration works to the toilets.

In 1956 the Company camp site moved from Dover to Charmouth

where it remained for four years. The site at Charmouth compared
to Dover was closer to the sea but perhaps a more difficult journey,
as this extract from Arthur Bowbeer states; "Memories of Camp are
many. When travelling by train to Axminster for Camp at
Charmouth (near my present home), the interchange time at
Wimbledon was only four minutes ... and our faithful Rolly Clark
'didn't think it funny' to heave and help with all the kit in/out of the
goods lift. He was heard to ask "Who thought-up this crazy journey?" - looking hard at me - but was the first to say 'Hey, Bow, -
isn't this smashing country' as we entered Dorset, and Camp." The
Officer meeting minutes comments that the 1956 camp Visiting
Officer was impressed by the spiritual side of camp and that discipline had been very good whilst the senior boys and NCO's
approved of the site.

Mike Wallace's thoughts on camp show the sacrifices made by the
staff and some of the time honoured -"tricks" played by boys and
staff alike. "Camp has to be mentioned if only for the fact that in
most work staff holiday allowances were two weeks often only one
with pay~ the Officers and others would give up one week to take us
away. In my first year I was told I had to obtain a Brailing spanner
and being very naive I tried to get one. The boys against Officers
football match started with eleven each side but once the Officers
were well in the lead the boys team increased in size to about twenty
when we won and left the pitch ."

 For the camp in 1958 the Officers meeting records "it was placed
on record that it had been a fair camp though meal parades had
lacked some of the customary discipline." A fuller record of the
same years camp was recorded in the annual report to the 1959 display which described the camp in the following glowing terms.
"Once again we camped at Charmouth on the borders of Dorset and
Devon, a jewel of a place, three minutes from the sea with the River
Char flowing at the bottom of the field, a place of health and vitality.
We arrived to find the camp layout not quite to our liking so on the
word 'go' each tent commander with the boys assigned to his tent
had to strike a tent and re-pitch it in the correct position. Well on the
word go it looked as if a hurricane had hit the camp, tents falling
everywhere, feverish activity by boys, and before you could say Jack

Robinson the first tent was completed and the boys of that tent reporting at the flag pole and proud as peacocks. Within an hour the whole camp had been re-pitched, a transformation in scene that will never be forgotten. 33 boys and 7 staff (including cook and other helpers) went to Camp 1958 and with us in Camp were our old friends the 3rd Mid-Surrey and the 128th London - a total of 69 boys and 14 staff. No pen picture of words can describe camp, it is an experience that lives for ever in the memory and no boy has taken full measure of the BB until he has been to camp. It may be of interest to you to know that enough bread and butter was eaten to cover a full size running track, 3½ hundredweight of potatoes were peeled and eaten, 50 gallons of milk and 56 gallons of porridge were spooned into the hungry mouths sweetened with 2½ hundredweight of sugar." To put these quantities into their metric equivalents that's : 177.8 Kilos of potatoes; 127 kilos of sugar; 227 litres of milk and 254 litres of porridge. Whilst on the subject of food at camp, there was always the difficulty of getting boys to eat what was good for them. As Arthur Bowbeer says "Liver, for example ... 'We don't like it Sir' ... but when Quartermaster Gordon Ferriman and cook George Blake served it as 'Liver and Bacon Lyonnaise" (or something like that), with stuffing all over it, every morsel disappeared."

The Inspecting Officer's report for the same camp is equally glowing, with the following comments:
Daily routine: Camp routine was a bit upset by the weather, and the muddy conditions prevailing, but none the less a proper system was maintained throughout.
Prayers: I witnessed the evening prayers, and I was struck with the reverence of the boys and the simple but effective methods adopted by the officers.
Cleanliness: Plenty of mud, which could not be helped , but the absence of litter was noticeable.
Cooking: The cook house was in a remarkably clean condition, well organized, and the food all clean and appetizing.
Other People: There were two Girls camps in the vicinity and these caused the officers some anxiety, but good, firm discipline was the order of the day and had it's effect.

A different view on the last comments comes from one of the senior boys at the Camp, John Ward ". In my last camp we went after lights out to meet the girls from a neighbouring camp , must have been at Charmouth , we were caught , but I'll pass a veil over the evening , we were caught coming back and we were confined to camp on our free day. We were given a good dressing down , peeled potatoes , but then played in the boys v staff football match which we won!"

Before we leave camp 1958 its interesting to note that it was filmed. However we don't know if a copy of that film is still in existence.

The following year's camp was also at Charmouth and the note in the officers meeting minutes after that camp is a bit like the proverbial curate's egg. "It was the fourth year at Charmouth. 38 boys from the 70th attended, plus 26 from the 3rd and 8 from 1st Kingsbridge. The 70th numbers were the highest for many years, including almost all the senior boys of the company. Weather, food and equipment were first class. The programme for the first time included free time for all in the evening (prior to that seniors had had some free time on three nights up to 8.15pm, a change on the early 1950's when no one was allowed out after tea). In spite of all this the general spirit was not good. Three 70th tents entered a 'let's be last' contest in the tent competition, but two later improved. Cpl Golder's tent came an honourable 2nd. Night discipline was variable, but poor all the time in certain tents.   More bad language was noted than in previous years. Having said all this, it now appears that we may have achieved more than in some years when the spirit was satisfactory. My personal opinion (Arthur Bowbeer) is that we should approach Mr.Rose (Captain 37th London) with a view to the syndicate finding a new site or if necessary go it alone." The minutes then note "There had been some doubts expressed as to the wisdom of holding a camp at all in 1960 but some Officers, on reflection, felt that we should do so and although this was not unanimously agreed, those dissenting stated that they would give Camp 1960 their support if it were held."

It is possible that the following incident recorded by Jack Fishpool may have happened at that camp. Jack, despite being an NCO was unusually at 16 a first time camper in 1959.   He records the incident as follows. "At summer camp with the 3rd Mid-surrey, the whole camp was ordered to fall in by a 3rd Mid Surrey Officer. He did not like our first fall in, (too slow or slovenly) so ordered us to fall out and in again. This happened a couple of times, so I shouted to the officer 'I'm fed up being messed about' and said I would sit down until he was satisfied with the falling in. I then sat down on the grass and watched whilst the Company fell out and fell in again. The Officer said it's only Jack having a tantrum ignore him. Everyone laughed except me. But after the parade a lot of the boys thought of me as a hero."

It is clear that the Officers were obviously unhappy with the camp overall as to threaten to stop camping would have been unheard of except in time of war. Speaking at a reunion in 1988 Arthur took a more rounded view of the night time antics as he was able to laugh and joke about the incidents involving certain boys paying unauthorized visits to the local Girls Life Brigade camp, and how he had to placate the GLB officers the day after. However, night time activity at camp was not always restricted to elicit nocturnal visits by the boys. Officer's supper was held after lights out and on one famous occasion, (probably camp in 1960) as Arthur Bowbeer recounts writing in 1998 "Lots of laughter as we relaxed together: flap of marquee suddenly opened by pyjama clad Ralph Price (no1 Tent Commander): 'Mr B., can the Officers please be quiet…the boys can't get to sleep.' The subtleties of that request will be lost on anyone who has not been to camp."

1959 was the last camp at Charmouth and it's interesting to note the views on those camps from two different old boys. John Ward wrote "Camps were at Charmouth, where the sea and wonderful beaches were much closer. Curiously, it is the sounds of Camp I remember most; sounds that still haunt me. Bugles playing the retreat at Sundown, the hiss of the lamps and the harmonium at evening prayers, the Last Post at lights out."

Whilst Alan Cadney wrote "There is an incident at Camp at Charmouth, Dorset near where I now live, somewhere between '57 and '59, which has always stuck in my mind.
I was drinking Ginger Beer from the bottle when Willy Ward pushed it into me and chipped a tooth. I was so angry with the sudden pain

and was preparing to hit him. I looked at him and he was just smiling in his way without a trace of malice or anything of the sort. He was just being his nice, gentle, genuine self and my anger disappeared instantly."

1960 saw a change in Camp site to Pett Level near Hastings. The site was different from Charmouth and the Company had the unusual situation of having to contact the Local Council (Battle RDC) and the local water company to get permission to have a water tank as there was no running supply to the site. The local farmer who rented the site out for the camp took a somewhat dismissive view as to the need for ready supplies of water   stating "Boys never did like washing anyway. Chuck them in the sea once a day!" He was however more helpful in providing straw for bedding in paliasses (no friendly donkey comments) at one shilling a truss , ten were needed for the whole camp. Whilst the fact that camp, as was the norm, in the 1950's and 60's was held in a working farm was illustrated by his request "we will need to move the sheep and lambs both out of , and back into, the field while you are there for dipping, so the six ridge tents nearest the sea should not be too close so as to impede the sheep" . Transport was again "the back of a lorry" by road after a detailed costing exercise comparing that with cost of British Rail from Tooting to Hastings which included two changes.   No consideration was given to the health and safety considerations or comfort of using the lorries.

The programme at Pett Level was similar to that of previous years, but the staff, mindful of what had happened in 1959, had more organized sports activities in the evening. There was also, perhaps a sign of the times, a ban on portable radios. In common with other camps of the period the camp visitation report stated that there was a high standard . "General tone was good and all seemed to be enjoying themselves…plenty of everything , cooking by calor gas , menu varies each day and plenty of it." The camp at Pett Level was a break with the long established fifty year old practice of either camping with or sharing the site on different weeks with the 37th London who remained at Charmouth.

One member of the Camp staff deserves a special mention and that is George Blake. George was the Camp cook throughout the 1950's and in 1960 the following camp equation was made.

4 meals = 1 day
7 days = 1 camp
12 camps = 1 George
1 George = 23,520 individual meals
-         No further comment is really needed!

Amongst the meals that George would have delivered were sausages and bacon, chipped and boiled potatoes ,peas , followed by plain duff and treacle sauce; brown stew , boiled potatoes ,peas , followed by plum duff and custard and roast lamb boiled potatoes , peas and carrots with plum duff and custard. Breakfast was always porridge followed by a fried variant (sausage ,bacon , spam or beans) on fried bread . Good cooking that perhaps with its high fat content may not always have met the ideal of the modern nutrionist.

One boy who was at camp throughout this period was Alan Rance and he recalls his camps as follows. "This was the only holiday for some boys. I remember that the cost was just £4! You could pay by weekly instalments if you liked!
Transport to the one-week camp was by removal/furniture lorry. Boys were packed into the lorry with their kit bags for a journey that must have taken many hours to the destination, Dover or latterly Charmouth [near Lyme Regis].

We slept in bell tents with up to 8 in each tent, sleeping like the spokes of a wheel with feet towards the central tent pole. Each tent had a nominated tent commander and a name. I remember at my last camp our tent being called the 'Winkle Shell' after my nickname!

It is perhaps the aromas of camp that linger most in my memory. The smell of hot chocolate drinks at reveille, the combined smell of the grass and the straw paliasses we slept on, and of course the not so pleasant smell of the latrines, holes in the ground where we took relief as quickly as possible.

Sounds too remain evocative: the 'strained' sound of the portable

organ churning out the hymns in the huge marquee, the hissing of the hurricane lamps at night and the sound of last post, signalling time to go to sleep supposedly!
There were many a night of high jinks when boys would creep out to visit other tents or even go off campsite into the local town. This all had to be done without alerting the prowling officers.

Once in the week there would be a compulsory march down to the sea for a dip. I suspect that this event was to make sure that we boys had a least one wash in the week!

A rota meant that on one day in the week you found yourself as an orderly. This involved washing up duties, peeling potatoes and other unexciting, but essential tasks.

There was great excitement however when we played 'Royalists and Rebels'. This was essentially a game of 'hide and seek' over several neighbouring fields. The mission was to capture your enemies' flag without being caught. Exhausting but memorable fun.
The last night at camp was always an emotional one with the singing of the hymn 'We thank thee Oh our Father before the memories fade… Many boys made their 'decision' on such a night, a pledge to follow a Christian way of life."

The Company displays in the late 1950's followed the pattern set under Bert Porter, with a Themed display operating on both a Friday and Saturday evenings in late April or early May to close the winter Session. The one exception was the 1959 Display which appears to have been a Saturday only affair and a traditional format. The displays were chaired on one of the two evenings, normally the Saturday by the Company Chaplain Rev. Edmund Gabb, whilst the Inspecting Officer was normally a local Company Captain or former officer of the Company. The first display of Arthur Bowbeer's Captaincy was a re-run of "The BB on Trial ", whilst subsequent productions - which is the best way of describing them included "Space pioneers", "Jubilee", "The British" and "Western Style". Throughout this period individual badges and certificates were not presented at the display but were presented on a separate awards evening a few weeks later. As in earlier years much work went into the production of the display both by the staff and boys, and both sessions were well attended as the boys depicted the various company activities in novel and innovative ways. Perhaps some of the most memorable sketches , and definitely the best used were some of the camp sketches that were recycled more often in future years, than editions of "only fools and horses" on the television. However they still maintained a freshness to them even forty years later. The display also produced a good source of funds for the Company with the adult entrance fee held at 1/6d (7½p) throughout the period, providing good value entertainment when compared to the 2007 comparative cost of just over a pound.

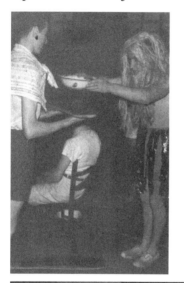 

The display wasn't the Company's only public performance as in 1960 they also undertook a concert in February of that year entitled

"Sevenomania". This production raised £20 for the church redecoration fund and included amongst other items such gems as "on the packed terraces", "Gentleman of the road " and "Studio a la Schmidt".

The Life Boys had their own programme throughout this period under the continuing leadership of Ivy Clark, and the interaction between the Company and the Life Boy group was limited to one or two meetings between the staff a year, and even the church tended to look upon them as two separate organisations as any meetings where the church called together the organisations the Life Boys were separately represented. However, this was not uncommon as throughout the Brigade at that time the Life Boys did their own thing and the Boys Brigade Company had their own programme, only mixing when they had to, but having separate displays and awards evenings.

After Camp at Bembridge on the Isle of Wight in 1961, Arthur Bowbeer confirmed to the Officers present at a staff meeting that he would be resigning from the Captaincy due to "increasing business responsibilities and that the decision was made with the greatest reluctance". Rolly Clark on behalf of the staff said " He recalled Mr Bowbeers' untiring and devoted service to the company over some fifteen years as an Officer and as Captain during the past six… and the loss to the Company would be incalculable." Despite resigning as Captain, Arthur continued to be involved in the Brigade as Battalion press and publicity officer and subsequently as Bible Class convenor which largely involved organizing the battalion scripture competition. He also assisted the Company as an instructor and on the camp staff in the 1970's, whilst serving in the Church as a Deacon until moving to Dorset in 1987.
Perhaps the natural successor to Arthur as Captain was Gordon Ferriman who had been in the Company at the same time as Arthur but had moved out of the district some years and had intended to resign on that basis back in 1955. He had remained with the Company at that time but he had now decided that he would need to sever his ties with the Company shortly which he did in 1962. So the new Captain was Peter Knights who had rejoined the staff in 1960 following a gap of four years out of the Company due to evening classes.

The Sixties (1961-69)

The appointment of Peter Knights to the captaincy of the company in September 1961 saw the company in good heart , company strength was 57 and a lifeboy team of 25. Peter was backed up by a experienced staff in the shape of Roly Clark , Gordon Ferriman (soon to leave in May 1962) and Fred Bateman . There were also experienced and successful instructors such as Brian Rance and Martin Nightingale . David Golder joined the staff in 1962 and others such as Peter Ellis , Will Ward and Ralph Price also became warrant officers first and then lieutenants. Extracts from Peter's first annual report to the 1962 Display gives a candid flavour of how the company was running in the early 1960's.

"Reflecting the Company work since last we met in this way would be very lengthy. I will endeavour to present to you a brief picture of the Company .Tooting village fayre was a high powered weekend in the halls and the company was privileged to take part in the sales of basketwork and Christmas cards. Senior boys and officers provided the night guards for the Fayre and also took part in the concert to close the Fayre"

"B.B Week commenced on the same day as our annual enrolment service, which was conducted by a previous company chaplain . We returned a total of £122 which was an increase on the previous year. Operation Goodwill enabled us this year to provide 22 older people with a food parcel and a sack of firewood each and our Carol singing , where we joined the GLB raised £10 for Spurgeon's homes."

"The company e'sprit-de-corps is high ......Attendances at Drill Parade and Bible Class have been below average and the result being that we stand little chance of achieving the battalion efficiency colour.... The band has had a difficult session and the ranks were depleted due to the loss of experienced players . However , new members joined the band and the process of rebuilding is their prime task. A further disappointment was in our football. Due to lack of support we were compelled to withdraw our first team from the Battalion league."

"First aid has enjoyed its most successful year . The weekly class has been well attended an a high standard of efficiency attained . In the sphere of competition we entered two teams into the battalion competition and were successful in coming first and second. Our team aim's to return with the London Trophy." The A team were in fact successful and won the company's first ever London trophy winning the first aid competition in 1962. This was in no small part down to the instructors as Peter goes onto say " My thanks to Messrs Rance, Ellis and Sale who impart their knowledge to the boys week by week and who are responsible for the high standard attained."

After the initial session company membership stabilised over the next three years with numbers being in the mid 40's (An average sized London company was at that time about 25 boys) and an unprecedented run of success occurred in London competitions as has already been mentioned the First Aid Trophy was won five times in seven years, the Athletics team also assisted the Battalion team to win the London Trophy but there was also success at gym winning the battalion competition four years in succession from 1963 and the London competition three years from 1964. It should be remembered that this success was at a time when to become London district champion you were the best company out of over 350 in the district . So to get two trophies in a year more than once in totally different disciplines was quite an achievement. This sequence of success seems even more remarkable when the view of a joint officers and NCO's meeting in January 1963 is taken into account . The meeting recorded Peter Knights stating "the company strength stands at 45...the future looks bleak unless we can get a good number of recruits."

In addition to the competition work , the Company still met four evenings a week in the winter (for instance in 1963 /4 the programme was Band -Monday, First aid -Tuesday, PT and Gym Wednesday, Drill & some badge classes on Friday). The programme stretched to five evenings in the summer . Football on Winter Saturdays, Cricket in the Summer. With the core meetings still being Drill and Bible Class. Attendance at these two remained compulsory throughout the period, and overall levels of attendance in the Winter session were 80% + in every Session. One change was the introduction of a new drill book and from the autumn of 1963 the company

The Company 1964 and first aid squad 1967 tagged up for another victory!

moved from drilling in fours to drilling in threes with the main differences being on the more complex movements in forming company when in two or three sections. The company adapted well to the new drill book winning the battalion "B" competition (two section drill?) during that session. The main weekly programme would be supplemented by an annual round of other activities such as an enrolment service early in the session ,BB week fund raiding collection in November (by 1963 this was raising over £200), operation goodwill distributing Christmas food parcels and chopped wood to the elderly , carol singing with the GLB for Spurgeon's Homes and the Company supper in January .

One issue that seemed to provoke a degree of controversy was smoking by boys outside the hall . In April 1963 the officers minutes record "Mr. Golder reported that a choir member had told him of the smoking and other irregularities that were occurring outside the hall on a Friday night, and he wanted to know if something could be done about it. After a great deal of heated discussion Mr. Knights decided that any boys caught smoking at any activity would be suspended forthwith." It would appear that the threat was sufficient as no-one was dismissed for this reason.

Bible Class was led from the BB Bible class handbook with speakers being a mix of company officers , old boys , church members and visiting officers from other companies. Amongst the series covered were "the King and the Kingdom", "The call and the covenant", "In the fullness of time", "God's Man" and "Facing Facts" Each series had a series of thirty talks which would provide ready made material from October to June of each year together with Bible readings for the day and the week and suggested hymns from the BB hymn book . The topics were generally thematic and ran through both the old and new testament. The summer months would be covered by a variety of ad hoc subjects. For part of this period the Reverend Alan Hughes as both minister and Company chaplain would also use the relevant theme from the Bible Class course for the monthly church parade. Bible class was at that time still held in what was then the junior hall ,the room is now the main hall of the church.

In addition to the monthly church parades , the company paraded twice a year with the battalion . These continued to be large scale affairs , particularly the whole battalion parades . Not all parades were all battalion parades as some of the smaller church's could not accommodate parades of that size (sometimes over 700 people) and thus half battalion parades would be organized where the battalion would parade to two different churches. One of the things about the church parades both in the sixties and earlier would be the individual company bands marching to the parade ground on one of the local commons from there own church , and as you approached the parade ground you could here the different bands playing as they came ever closer to the mutual meeting place. The battalion was fortunate to have in addition to many bugle bands , fife & drum bands (74th and 83rd) and brass bands (88th and 99th). This meant that for the parade to the host church there was an array of music played as the bands combined. Co-ordinating this was no mean feat but was managed with skill.

Another occasion where the battalion came together with good musical effect was for a Massed Band tattoo in Battersea Park in June 1963 , the 70th were one of 16 bugle bands which took part . The event was in aid of the Freedom from Hunger campaign and the Programme was as follows:-

Retreat- played by mass bugle bands
The Old Warrior- Brass bands
Z cars theme- Drum and fife bands
Joffre and St George- Bugle bands
Marching through Georgia- Massed bands
Abide with me - Brass and fife bands.

The event finished with Last post being played by buglers from the 70th , 79th and 27th. It is estimated that about 200 boys would have taken part in that event. A similar event with similar numbers was held in 1965 to mark the renaming of the battalion to the Wandsworth battalion following Local government re-organisation.

The strength of the company band varied in the early 1960's , in 1962 for instance the officers' minutes record that "because of a very bad start resulting in our not being able to enter the band competition." There was also discussion in the same year again about converting to a fife band which was dismissed as not being suitable. However , despite this and the strong competition from the other company's in the battalion the company was able to win the band competition in 1964 and the bugle team competition in 1965, after coming second the previous year which was followed in the same session a very good third place in the final of the all London Bugle team, demonstrating that the company's band work was still up to the mark.

The 1960's was a period of change for the Brigade as a whole and the 70th were not exempt from these changes. The Haynes report published in 1964 changed the fundamental structure of the Brigade bringing together the Life Boys and the BB company into one organisation and dividing the latter into two elements the company and senior sections. Together with this introduction of the three tier system , there were changes to the uniform with by the end of the sixties the Pill box being condemned to history , some company's adopting a new full uniform , based on blue shirts and no blazers and a radical change to the badge system .The speed of change was such that the Brigade nationally published regularly updated guides to national developments in order that Companies knew where they were with regard to the changes in ages , uniform and badge awards. One of the changes which the three tier system brought in , or in particular the change of the Life Boys to the junior section was the introduction of Lady Officers although back in the 1960's it was quite clear that "Those appointed for duty in the Company and senior sections shall be men. Those appointed for duty in the junior section may be men or women." The regulations were quite clear that the captaincy at that time was a male preserve "Every Company, whether of one, two or three sections, must be under the leadership of a Captain who is a man over the age of 20." It was many years later that women were able to become officers in any section or Company captain. Something that has been implemented in many places but not within the 70th. Peter Knight comments that "During this period several of the staff attended the Brigade Council Meetings at both Cambridge and also Southampton and shared in the discussions appertaining to both "Haynes" and also the proposed new uniforms. I cannot remember the actual comment on the uniform proposals that were expressed by Rolly Clark but they were not very complementary as were the others who were with me."

The 70th embraced the new three tier structure, which was optional for seniors, enthusiastically with a formal ceremony being held on the 17th September 1965 to inaugurate the company into the new structure only thirteen days after the structure had been approved by Brigade Council (The national BB governing body) . The new structure of juniors 8-11 ; Company 11-15 and Seniors 15-19 whilst emphasizing the unity of the Brigade which the old Life Boys and BB company did not did have its problems with the divorcing of the senior boy away from the younger company age, and the fact that this split was optional meant that with some companies opting for a traditional set up of a company section covering all ages from 11 to 18, there was a diversification within the Brigade that weakened the retention of the senior members. In addition to the three official BB sections the 70th started in the late 1960's an unofficial under 8's group the blue imps.

Some of the changes and difficulties that the new structure brought in particularly the company and senior section split were highlighted in Peter Knights annual report to the Company Display in April 1966. "It was in mid-September following the Company's Recruiting Campaign that an inaugural service was held in the church, re-constituting the 70th London as a Boys' Brigade Company with a Junior and Senior sections. We give thanks to God for the many parents and friends who came and supported us on that occasion and who still show their interest in all that we as a Company undertake.
Although this report is concerned mainly with the Company and Senior sections, I would at this point make mention of the Junior section which is so vital in the function of any Company. During the past session there has been a closer liaison between the Company and Section maintained by regular visits at the section· meeting by the Company Captain, with an active participation in the activity of the section, which in turn has helped the younger boys to realise more easily, that they are members of and belong to something bigger than just the section. We again give thanks to God for the staff of this section and for their loyalty and untiring service week by week for the benefit of the section, the company and the Advancement of Christ's Kingdom.

It is our constant prayer that this section may continue to expand and grow and that many boys all continue their service into the Company. The company session started with 40 boys on the roll after the transfer, of 11 senior members into the newly formed section.

Although the numbers were good, the change of structure within the company very soon began to show it's effect. New N.C.Os. were appointed, being made responsible for a squad assisted where necessary by the squad officer. It became apparent however that this session we lacked something we had in previous years. Looking back one can say that without a doubt, the senior members with their particular and established stability presented now a more junior company for working and what was now an immaturity within the ranks in matters of discipline and control. This effect quite naturally tends to show itself upon the drill standard attained and which in fact has been lower than for some years.

The programme re-arrangement produced yet another factor to be taken, into account, this time by the various company classes held throughout the week. In every activity without exception there has been a tendency for the boy to 'give up' when the activity appears to demand a little more effort, either physically or mentally. This sort of reaction makes for running a class or instructing a particular subject very difficult indeed."

Despite the above company was still able to attract recruits one of those who joined the 70th in the 1966 was Neil Pheasant, later to be captain, how he joined and what happened next are now described by him. "It was my Mum's idea! You just did not say "no" to my Mum. She invited Curly (Peter Knights, the Captain) round for a cup of tea as I recall and that was that. I have got to admit I was not keen to start with but the boys were very friendly. The first night was a Drill Parade just a week or so before the Annual Display. A lad called Robert Bristow, whose Dad owned a paper-shop in Gorringe Park Avenue, walked with me down to the church halls. It was Mick Bartlett, Tony Foard, David Carmichael and Martin Hughes who were the NCOs then and they really made me welcome.

That first night really sticks in my memory. I felt a little bit in awe of the discipline and the need to clean uniform etc. Rolly Clark inspected me, calling me "mate" and telling me that my hair needed a lot of brush and comb. I was standing next to a young lad called Stephen Lovegrove - somewhere near one of the Beadle boys. Stan was skinny as a rake, but his big brother, Les, was like a brickhouse. I got to watch the drill session as Fred Bateman put them through their paces. Then there was some pretty spectacular gym practice for the display. Why did I stay? I guess BB intrigued me. A bit scary, but it demanded something. Besides, no-one had ever called me "mate" before. You could just sense the friendliness, even through the strong discipline. I just went home and asked Mum to buy me a brush and comb!"

"It was Pete Ellis who taught me all the basic BB things about "The Object", "Motto", how to salute etc. Because I was starting at the end of the winter session rather than the beginning I think I was the only one in his "recruits class". We met in the primary hall using those tiny chairs that were very easy to get stuck in. He was a patient man! All the officers were all the finest Christian men. What a blessing that was to a young lad whose Dad was disabled and always away in some hospital or another."

Neil then describes the delights of uniform cleaning and wearing when the pill box was still in being and had not yet, which it would in 1970 be replaced by the "thunderbirds" style hat. This is going to sound "sad" to today's Boys, but I used to really enjoy cleaning my uniform and trying to make the best of it - all part of the esprit de corps of my "Squad". It was a right palaver too. Uniform cleaning kit was extensive. I think Mum started to think BB was not such a great idea after all. Starting at the top there was the Pillbox hat. It had chrome numbers "70" which could be slipped off. They had to be polished with Brasso - simple enough. The big challenge was getting the two white braid bands perfectly white. Rubber bands could be slipped each side of them to protect the edges and then you could use an old toothbrush to apply a generous layer of Meltonian cream - a tennis shoe whitener. The trick was carefully removing the rubber bands at the right time to ensure a nice crisp edge. The black serge of the rest of the hat would then be brushed spotless.
 Next came the haversack, which HAD to be washed and ironed each week. The problem was it had brass fittings which were

stitched in. Trying to polish those ALWAYS made the white material mucky. No problem - just get Mum to unpick all the stitching and sew in a few brass poppers. Then you could clean the brass bits away from the haversack, only putting the whole thing together at the last minute. Then the belt. Brown leather strap, and brass buckle and fittings. Masses of toothbrush and duster work again and a lot of Brasso. Both sides of the buckle had to be polished TOTALLY. Mr Ellis always checked! Once I became a Sergeant I had a cross-belt to clean as well - about three times the leather and a whole load of extra brass fittings!

A lot of Boys came unstuck when it came to their BB buttonhole badge. Often forgotten, not always cleaned, or just not lined up properly, it could lose vital points in the Squad competition. The whole thing was set off with a clean white shirt, black tie, black blazer and trousers and black shoes. Dark socks were essential!

One vital detail remained. Pleats! The back of the blazer had to be gathered under the belt into two equidistant pleats. Before Drill Parade started, or on church parade or other big event, all you could see where dozens of groups of two Boys "doing" each others pleats. Of course, I enjoyed more than uniform cleaning. I was a bit of slow starter when it came to the activity side of things but things like First Aid, Communications (Morse code etc), and Expedition all held their attractions.

My BIG hate was cross-country running. We HAD to do it at camp. One cross-country run could wipe out a whole year's good experiences. I always came back from camp vowing to leave the Company before the new session started - I never did though."

The subject of uniform is something that would be discussed by the Brigade as a whole over the 1960's until the compromise of keeping the old belt and haversack with the new style hat. However, some of this could have gone in a radical revamp which involved a white plastic belt, nylon haversack and cape!. Fortunately the voting on this uniform nationally was so close 887 company votes to 886 that the idea was dropped.

For much of the sixties the 70th retained a strong nucleus of senior boys, perhaps because of the emphasis on the Duke of Edinburgh's award scheme and a steady stream of 70th boys made there way to

either Buckingham or St James Palace to receive their Gold awards, in 1963 Ray Parker and Will Ward received their awards and in 1965 they were joined by Michael Davis, Brian Newman and Roy Norris by 1968 there were ten 70th
 Gold award winners. All of whom would have done all three stages (bronze, silver and Gold) and the fifty mile trek across wild country. Mike Wallace who was with Ray Parker and Will Ward on their Gold expedition describes that they sometimes did not always go to plan "I, Ray Parker, Willy Ward and three other boys from other company within our battalion did the Dartmoor walk our leaders name was Jeff from the 80th(?) All went well until the second to last day when Jeff had no energy and was sweating badly we had to carry his load and him, when we arrived back home he was rushed to hospital having double pneumonia he did eventual get better."

Much of the expedition training work would have been done over the summer whilst the Company would also have been preparing for the annual athletics events . Extracts from the local press show that although the company normally won the battalion event . They did not often win a lot of individual events again showing the strength of the Company in depth in achieving both a full team and getting boys through to the finals with good scoring results. This is illustrat-ed by a postcard sent by Brian Rance to Peter Knights who was at

Company 1966

Clacton at the time showing the 1963 results. "Athletic Results 1st 70th 109, 2nd= 79th and 74th 86,4th 88th 75, 5th 28th 58, 6th 118th 43 etc etc . Event winners Rowe -Discus over 16 ; Davis -440 yards (14-16) . A fine team effort -only two winners medals out of 45. A weakened team but reserves and second string fought for 5th and 6th we finally got home with 4th, 2nd and 2nd in the relay" The battalion win in 1963 was the last of seven consecutive wins going back to the 1950's, but the trophy was regained in 1965 and 1969.

The Company had taken part in a number of battalion band items in the annual London District display at the Royal Albert Hall, however the company had never presented a solo item . However in 1964 the company had its first item "Life in their hands" described in the programme as "the history of Artificial respiration and how it can be put to good effect." Planning for an item like this took some time and the original idea of the first aid item was discussed in August 1963 originally using the concept of a "hit and run" scene, the concept changed and despite the fact there was no guarantee that an item however well conceived would get past the scrutiny of the London district display committee and be showcased in the display work continued on it. The item was originally submitted in September 1963, and the item accepted in December, and involved a commentated sequence on how artificial respiration had changed over the centuries with the boys in full period costume with other props including bellows and barrels. The item was extremely well received and a note after the display from the London Secretary Gerald Walker highlights this "From many people I have heard that they considered your item to be the best in the show and I hope that you will pass on to Boys and all concerned the appreciation and thanks of the London Committee for an excellent performance." The item was also well received outside the district with requests from Cardiff, Northampton, Cleethorpes, Dunfermline, Renfrewshire, Glasgow and Nigeria for the script.

Following the success of the 1964 item, a further item was accepted by the display committee for the 1966 display, this item entitled "Bouncing through history" Was based on a history of ball games from the stone ages, Egyptian, Roman, through to the World cup final which was to be held at Wembley two months later however

London Display item 1964

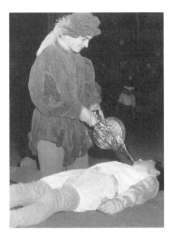

London Display items 1966 and 1968

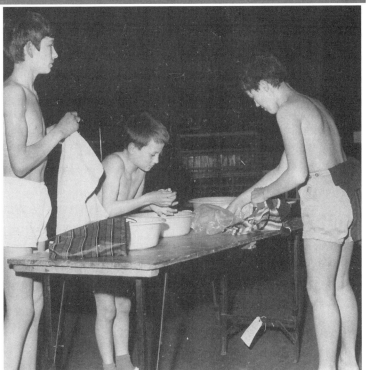

despite England reaching the final in the display item the lights went out with England drawing but on the attack . All that appears to have been missing was the voice of Kenneth Wolstenholme "They think it's all over". The 70th also took part in the massed bugle band item in the same display playing the marches "Slow march no2, New London and Carronvale". One the members who took part in the 1966 display was Neil Pheasant who comments about his involvement as follows "Royal Albert Hall Displays were always a highlight and a reminder that we were a part of something really big. Within a few weeks of joining I was running across the arena of that enormous amphitheatre taking part in a "display" of the history of soccer. Well it was 1966 and it was World Cup year."

The 70th were back in 1967 as First aid duty team and provided a third item in 1968 this team with long standing camping partners the 3rd Cheam (formerly 3rd Mid Surrey) showing the detail of a day at camp- entitled A recipe for Camp. The sketch was a series of narrations with boys carrying out the functions such as erecting the tents or tent inspection, orderlies etc. The sketch involved judicious use of spot lights to get the desired affect on the large Albert Hall Arena.

Thorough out the nineteen sixties the Company continued to hold the annual display with two appearances Friday and Saturdays. The theme would vary year by year sometimes as in 1963 recycling old themes such as "the BB on trial or in 1967 the theme was "in the beginning". This display together with later displays showed the new three section nature of the company with items from all three sections, rather than separate Life Boy and Company displays which had been the pattern in previous years. However, it clear from the officers minutes that the displays were very thorough affairs designed to "convince parents that the Boys' Brigade was playing a useful part in their sons upbringing and that we were achieving the object.". One thing that did vary from year to year was whether the display included the presentation of awards or not. It was not unusual for this to take place slightly later in the year in combination with a parents evening.

The general standard of the display work was high during this time as the attached extract from the inspecting officer's (Keith Woolcott captain 28th London) report for 1965 shows.

"1. The opening Parade was good, the steadiness of the Boys was very commendable. On the Inspection I found the standard of turn-out good, apart from the odd buckle not really clean and the caps not whitened, especially the button. Generally the main fault is of clean uniform not properly worn.

2. Drill. This was very good, and all Boys seemed to have a grasp of the various movements. One noticeable fault was knees not being raised while marking time. But on the whole I think Mr. Bateman congratulated on getting the Drill up to this standard

3. Band. Needless to say, I expected this to be good, and so it was. My only criticism is that the time was a little too slow.

4. First Aid. A well produced item, and full of interest for the spectators,knowing how difficult it is to put on a really good First Aid show, I was very impressed.

5. Vaulting and Ground Work. This was very good indeed, and the general quality of the work is of a high standard.

6. Parallel Bars. Always an impressive item, and I thought the squad did extremely well, my congratulations to their Instructor. The lighting effects added much to this item.

7. A day in Camp. A good idea, but somehow this item did not come up to the standard of the others, and I felt that not enough thought or practice had gone into it.

Taken as a whole, I thought the Display was very good, and I am sure the outlook for next session is very bright".

The staffing of the Life Boys, subsequently the Junior Section changed during the decade . The first major change was in 1963 when Ivy Clark "The little lady in the Tricorn hat retired after some 25 years of service, 24 of which were as Leader in Charge of the Section. She was succeeded by Will Ward, who became the first officer in charge of the Junior Section. Another long standing retiree was Vera Bowbeer who retired in 1966 after 12 years of service and in the last few months with the conversion of the Lifeboys to the Junior Section became the first 70th lady officer. The life boys and junior section programme continued pretty much as in previous years with a mix of games, badge work, skills and a regular spiritual programme. In the mid 1960's the evening moved to a Friday so that all three sections met on the same night with the juniors coming at 6.30pm before the Company and Senior Sections met at 8.15pm. The pre juniors or blue imps meeting on a Tuesday from 6.15pm to 7.00pm.

The change to the three section structure meant that boys were pro- moted to the Company section at 11 rather than nearer 12. This ini- tially affected junior section numbers but this appeared to be a tem- porary blip writing in 1967 Will Ward commented that "Over the past two months the influx of recruits has increased, the number now on the roll being 32." He goes on to say "In the general work of the section, the achievement scheme has played a valuable part .It has stimulated interest, not only among the boys but also among many parents and we do indeed thank those who have shown so much interest and have encouraged the boys in this sphere" The junior boys also took part in sporting activities such as the battalion sports at Woodfield recreation ground and regular Saturday football although with little success, however "The most pleasing feature being, that, they have had a good sporting spirit, and have never given up trying, no matter how the game was going."

During the mid sixties there were a number of changes to the Company and Senior Section staff. Martin Nightingale who had acted as a band instructor moved to Plymouth in 1963 .Brian Rance who had been the Athletics and Duke of Edinburgh's award instruc- tor moved out of the area in 1966, the same year that Dave Golder left as a lieutenant followed by Ralph Price, Will Ward and Rolly Clark in 1967. Rolly was the last of the pre war officers and left after 29 years unbroken service to the boys in the company, a time span only surpassed by the Company founder. The staff changes were not all one way with Michael Davis and Brian Newman becoming lieutenant's in 1968 and George Bartlett an officer in 1969. Brian and George were predominantly Junior section officers, with Brian becoming officer in charge.1969 also saw two other jun- ior section officers move out of the area Barry Rowbotham and Martin Hughes.

The loss of five experienced staff members in just over twelve months affected the operation of the company. During this period the company and senior section strength was on average in the 30's low historically by the 70th's standards but higher than the London average. The changes in the company are reflected in some of the extracts from the officers' minutes with the October 1967 minutes reflecting that. "The company had withdrawn from the Battalion and London Cross Country events due to lack of entrants" and later in the same meeting "Band attendance had been very bad, several boys were not attending due to local circumstances. Mr. Knights made the suggestion that the company band practice could include members of the Girls Brigade band." Despite these apparent difficulties the company was still able to carry out a full programme of activities during it's sixtieth session including the Christmas activities of operation Goodwill and Carolling for Spurgeons homes.

Preparations for the Company's diamond jubilee in 1968 were pretty much on the lines of the fiftieth year celebrations. Including a reunion, battalion parade and display. The display like many others of the period was held on the Friday and Saturday evening and from the correspondence received from old boys and the list of signatures on the special brochure there was a good turn out of old boys going back to the early days of the Company. The display included junior section items and guest appearances from both the 3rd Mid-Surrey and the 1st Farnham .The inspecting officer on the Saturday Gerald Walker the then London Secretary gave a commendably glowing report "I felt the programme was full of interest and variety but at the same time items were comfortably short and to the point. I mentioned in particular in my remarks the Drill performance of the Company and I would like to repeat what I said that it was well done and smartly executed, when bearing in mind the somewhat limited space. All those concerned are to be commended. I would remind the Boys of the importance of lifting their feet and when at attention keeping their hands in the correct position and their shoulders back. It was obvious that all members were enjoying themselves and at the last when all the 'Old Boys' were· on-parade, it was a very satisfying sight I am sure for you and your colleagues. It is always a great thrill to present a Queen's Badge and to present four in one evening is quite an occasion, and I do congratulate you on the wide and interesting programme which you have presented to the Boys during the session. Despite the difficulties which you outline I feel that you have much to be proud of and can feel satisfied with a job well done." The comment about difficulties alludes to observations made in Peter Knights' annual report to the same display extracts from which follow

"The 60th Session of the Company has probably been one of the most difficult in the long history of work among boys here in the 70th. A very mixed spirit has prevailed throughout the membership, a spirit which has been at times without the slightest trace of enthusiasm toward the work of the Company. Despite the various difficulties and setbacks, we have engaged upon a vigorous programme... September and a company strength of 44 boys including 6 Seniors an increase of 11 mainly promotions from the Junior Section....With the winter session under way with activities of Band, P.T. and Gym, First Aid as the main programme supporting the two major meetings of Bible Class and Drill Parade the company settled to it's work of preparation for the coming Battalion and District events. It was however a great disappointment to us all, that because of the irregularity at the classes by some boys and the eventual dismissal from the class that we unable to defend any of the trophies we gained last year... The company strength today is 37 having dismissed 13 boys from the ranks for one reason or another and accepted 4 new recruits to offset these losses.

It is with these numbers we plan to grow and strengthen as we look forward into the future starting yet another chapter in the life and work of the 70th." Despite the obvious tone of disappointment in the report there was an upside 5 boys being baptized, and a good size Junior section of 38 boys . The Diamond jubilee concluded with a reunion in December which was on similar lines to the 1958 golden jubilee but with a buffet replacing the sit down meal and plenty of time for recollections. On the following day the battalion paraded to the church and all three of the surviving captains took part in the service which was led by John Edbrooke, the London Field officer.

The company kept track of a number of its former members through the work of the old boys association which continued to meet throughout the 1960's . Meeting one evening a week for badminton and other related activities and the regular monthly bible Class . The association worked closely with the company during much of this period particularly with the senior section who had the option of attending either the Old boys Bible Class, company bible class or church on a Sunday. The Old boys cricket team ran throughout the period, whilst the football team was more intermittent. Other activities included car rallies and ladies evenings The association also provided assistance with stewarding at displays and other occasions.

1969 appears to see the senior section merge back in with the company section giving a structure similar to that which had existed before 1965. This year also saw the adoption of a new badge system which replaced the old large BB activity badges and certificate system which ran throughout the six or seven years of a boy's service in the Company with a basic or target award and then a new bronze coloured system largely covering the same topics as the old scheme but with three levels at first, second and third stage. The latter stage broadly equated to the Duke of Edinburgh's bronze award and getting the right combination of badges at second and third stage would entitle a boy to a new award the Presidents Badge. The award system assumed that at the age of 15/16 a boy would have obtained his Presidents Badge and would be working towards his Duke of Edinburgh's silver award and/or his Queens Badge.

The 1969 display was topically titled "seven-naughts" and had a space theme. The display reverted to being on just the one occasion the Saturday night with both sections parading. The session seems to have been one of recovery with company numbers up from 27 at the start of the session to 41 at the end. Described as "a goodly number in this day of difficulty in retaining the interest of the boy." There was also a recovery in terms of competitions winning the battalion squad efficiency (Squad drill) competition and coming second in first aid and football.

One summer activity which continued constantly throughout the 1960's was camp . The 70th continued to camp with the 3rd Mid surrey (3rd Cheam after 1965) at a variety of sites. 1961 and 62 saw the first "overseas" visit to the Bembridge/ Whitecliff Bay area of the Isle of Wight. The 1962 camp also saw a new company joining the 70th and the 3rd the 181st London based in Clapham Park. After this camp the Nco's suggested that "there was too much responsibility attached to being a tent commander's job so could they have a free night/nights out" The staff response was somewhat predictable. "This was ridiculous". The 1962 daily routine would again be familiar to boys from earlier generations with Reveille still at 6.30am with washing by tents. A note on this in the camp orders has the telling three words in red capitals "EVERYONE WILL WASH", tent inspection was fitted in around washing with inspection at 7.40am, Breakfast was 8.10am followed by morning prayers, the day would then be split into morning, afternoon and evening sessions with lunch at 1pm and tea at 5 pm. Tuesday was a free day with boys allowed out unsupervised between breakfast and tea, however this was followed by the camp cross country at 6.30 in the evening. Evening prayers were held every evening after supper at 9.00pm. Camp sports were not undertaken in tents but in redrawn groups. In 1962 the nine boys tents were drafted into six teams . In addition to football, rugby netball was also played and a boys team played the staff at both games, and a camp sports was held on the Wednesday afternoon.

The following year all three companies again camped together at Teignmouth . The first camp in Devon. There was another change with the company travelling down overnight on the Friday by coach, coach was to become the preferred method of travel until the late 1970's. The change in venue and significant increase in cost from £3.19s 6d to £4. 7s 6d, did not act as a deterrent to the boys.

1964 saw another camp in Devon at Exmouth with over 100 officers and boys on the camp from the three companies this increase in the size led to some complaints from the NCOs "That the camp was too big and blamed this for the apparent lack of spirit and reverence" . One programme item that was enjoyed by the seniors was the night hikes. The following year saw a smaller camp with the 181st camping with the 83rd London and yet another change of site with the first camp at Swanage which was visited again in 1966. This camp was attended by just over 50 boys and staff, a significant reduction when compared to that of 1964 .However the programme in this year was not greatly different from the 1950's or earlier .One change that did occur in 1966 was in the post camp programme where rather than continuing to meet to continue badge work there was an informal programme throughout August.

The camp site moved again in 1967, not through dissatisfaction with the Swanage site but because it was unavailable and the site changed to near Plymouth. The following year saw a further change to Weston near Sidmouth where the company again camped in 1969. This rotation of sites added to the variety for the boy both for bathing and on free day but did add to the logistical problems particularly for the Quartermaster in contacting and finding new suppliers of food to keep a hungry camp fed. In the absence of refrigerators and freezers milk, bread and fresh food would be delivered by the local suppliers on a daily basis.

The camps in the 1960's were not without incident as Peter Knights comments "The year we camped at Venn Farm and on the one free day during the week the Pastor Alan Hughes myself and Roger Newman drove along the coast to visit the G.B.Camp at Bridport. Roger`s reason to visit was in some way different to ours, but no further comment."

"The 1966 Camp at Swanage and being "football world cup year" the evening sports programme was centred on a football competition.The highlight was the final on visitors day when the winners were presented with the Camp World Cup (made up of an enamel mug fixed to an enamel porridge bowl and duly labelled etc. Medals were presented being different coloured caps from dis-used pop bottles. The presentation was made by Miss Hazel Bowbeer to the great delight of many. "

"The 1967 Camp at Weston meant that we had an overnight coach journey which was something of a novelty, and can you believe it slung between the coat racks was the company canoe which had been made by the crafts class in an earlier time and had been stored in the loft. It was well used during the week and enjoyed by all." (some 40 years later the canoe is still in the loft!, although its fitness has not been recently tested.)

As in previous years camps were inspected by an officer from the local area on behalf of the Brigade nationally to ensure that the standard of the camps were maintained invariably the comments made

Camp
Group photographs from 1965, 1969 and 1968. The group
photos show the change in the make up of the company during
the late 1960's.

by the inspecting officers were favourable with observations such as "The ideal Boys' Brigade Camp, very well run, fine BB spirit" (1964 report), "The tone of this camp between officers and boys was very good"(1966) and "A normal BB routine was being followed, with provision for morning and evening prayers, and the general tone and discipline of Camp was good, varied menu, good programme of games and activities" (1962).

Each years camp had a different programme of evening prayers often based around ideas that were familiar to the boys these would include the Duke of Edinburgh's award scheme(1961), bugle calls (1966) and the Good camper (1967). These talks taken by different officers each day would challenge the boys as to their lifestyle and the claims of Christ and the Christian life in particular.

The changes in the Brigade throughout the 1960's had affected the company over the same period and in many respects the company in late 1969 was different to that of 1960. Although the programme would have been recognizable both in terms of weekly content and seasonal routine (recruiting, enrolment, Christmas activities, company supper, competitions, display, Summer session and camp), much of the confidence that came from the familiar old structure both in terms of sections, uniform and badge structure was gone. There were other issues as well in that the make up of the company was changing with a good proportion of the boys now being Caribbean migrants an issue that was causing some problems in some companies in the battalion to the extent that an attempt was made to discuss this specific issue without success at more than one battalion council. The acceptance of boys from whatever their background does not appear to have been a problem with the 70th.

There were also other difficulties in the late 1960's in particular part time jobs a result of the gradual raising of the school leaving ages and a more affluent society in general as Peter Knights explains "One of the problems in the late 60`s was that of boys having to work in various stores not only on Saturday but also now on Friday to make sure that they could still work on the Saturday. This meant some hard choices which in some cases saw our numbers decrease, but we survived."

The Seventies 1970-1980

The start of the 1970's saw the 70th numerically speaking at perhaps it's lowest numbers since the Second World War, with a Company section of some 24 boys and 18 Juniors. The numbers for the Company section was at the average strength for the battalion, which was still by some degree the largest in London. The BB in fact was expanding in Tooting with two new companies opening in the area in the early seventies - the 57th at Tooting Methodist and the 8th London at All Saints, Franciscan Rd. The experiment with the three tier structure of Senior, Company and Junior section had failed with all companies in the battalion bar one reverting to including the seniors in with the company section. The pill box hat was about to finally disappear with the sailor hat for junior boys to be replaced by the "thunderbirds" cap. There was perhaps a note of despondency at the start of the decade reflected in Peter Knights Captain's report to the 1970 Church AGM when he wrote: "The session commenced with a total of 47 boys on the company roll. The strength now stands at 26 boys with an average attendance of 20 boys. The company activities have also shown a decline in popularity with only a small percentage of boys attending. The reasons for many of the losses within the ranks, is the fact that the boys concerned were not prepared to fulfil the obligatory demands of the organisation, therefore being discharged from the Company. Others, with no real reason at all just wanted to leave. These facts are discouraging and tend to make the work of the Company more exacting."

Compared to any other period since the Second World War, the company staff was also limited and these resources were further depleted with the sudden death of Fred Bateman in July 1970. Peter Ellis also moved away in 1970 leaving the company section with just two officers. The company was to run on diminished staff resources throughout the 1970's with Tony Foard becoming a Lieutenant in 1971, but leaving the following year. Neil Pheasant became on officer in 1975 but Mick Davies left in 1977. With the Junior Section, Brian Newman left in 1971 and George Bartlett became officer in charge being joined by Jim Ballard in 1977.

Despite the staffing situation the Company still took part in a full range of activities including being part of a battalion item in the 1970 London district display. This item was based on the Brigade International and it was perhaps apt that the battalion should put on this item as the battalion, as well as the 70th, had by that time a much more diverse membership even when compared to five years earlier. The company also took part in a number of externally organised expedition based activities such as the Cleveland Hike and a night patrol organised by the battalion.

The programme for the winter session of 1970-71 saw little significant difference from that of earlier years. Bible Class was on Sunday's at 10.00am, with church parades now being on the first Sunday of each month. Band was at Franciscan Road school on Mondays, Pt and Gym on Tuesdays, First aid on Thursdays and drill on Fridays, with the junior section preceding and badge classes and club room following. Football was on Saturday. Subs were 1/- (5p) a week, equivalent to 55p a week at 2007 prices. The session saw the Company's one competition success of the decade winning the under 15 football league. The Junior Section was also successful in their league as well. Both teams had presentations made to them in the 1971 display.

Bible Class continued to be the mainstay of Christian Education within the company section and again as in previous decades the BB Bible class handbook was the basis of the talks, with hymns from the BB hymn book. However, there was one change from earlier years which perhaps reflected the changes within the church, and that was the significantly lower number of speakers at Bible Class from the church. The full rota was filled by the staff speaking more frequently and by using speakers from other companies.

Since the company had started in 1908 it had had no part of the church or halls that it could regard as its own base or headquarters. In September 1970 this changed when following a request from Peter Knights the deacons agreed to what was then called "room no 4", becoming the company HQ something that it has remained to this day. Strangely this is the room that had earlier been the base for

the then discontinued Christian Endeavour group and from which the company had been "banned" from in
the 1950's.

The company also continued to hold the company supper every year although there were sometimes surprises. At the 1975 supper there was an appearance by "Stiff Pilchard and the Shaddocks" otherwise known as the company NCO's . There is believed to be a tape of this or an associated performance in existence which fortunately has never been commercially released, probably to protect the reputation of those involved. The menu for the same supper was again traditional fare. In other years the supper would be themed, for instance the 1976 supper had a cowboy theme with games entitled "Bulls eye", "Round up" and "Pony express"

Throughout the 1970's the main source of income for the company apart from Company subscriptions was the annual BB week collections. In addition to the traditional card collections from friends and church members and donations from Old Boys, sponsored activities such as table tennis and walks were used to good effect. For instance in 1970 £181 was raised, compared to a target of £150. The amount collected rose to £306 in 1976 and £420 in 1977. On paper a significant increase in the sum collected, but in practice a figure that did not quite keep pace with the rapid inflation of the 1970's.

BB week was not the only fundraising event held, and during the seventies the company took part in a number of fundraising activities both for its own funds, but also for other organizations. One such event was the 1971 "distrek" appeal which was a fund raising appeal both for the church and the London district of the Boys' Brigade. Events were held throughout London and the battalion had its own event on Tooting Common, but the 70th held its own event on Figges Marsh on 26th June. A total of 929 laps were completed by the 59 participants which included a number of church members and the minister and his wife (David and Valerie Reddaway), who were also the largest fundraisers. The total sum raised was in excess of £270.

The money raised from BB week and other activities were used to fund the regular activities of the company. One regular expense year by year was the hire of football pitches, normally on Figges Marsh. Apart from the success of 1971 the company team had mixed fortunes both at home or on their travels to Wandsworth, Tooting and Clapham Commons. There is a complete record of one season 1973/74 and the home record that season was remarkably good with six wins out of six games. However the away record was not so good with only two wins out of six - obviously the team did not travel that well. Goal scoring was not a problem with 70 scored. However 40 were conceded. What is clear from the reports is that the result was secondary to the desire to have a good game regardless of the result.

Throughout the 1970's the Company annual display continued, although now on just the one night - Saturday. As in previous years this showcased the work of all sections of the Company and allowed parents and friends the opportunity both to support the boys and see some of the activities undertaken by the company over the last year, and to see the badges gained and individual company trophies such as the "esprit d'corps" presented.

One new trophy presented from 1971 was the Bateman cup for the 70th boy who had the best overall mark in the battalion scripture exam. This was first presented to Vernon Sore. The Bateman cup succeeded an earlier trophy presented by Rolly Clark which disappeared in the late 1960's. The display programme would reflect the regular activities such as drill, gym, first aid and band, (the latter was sometimes with the Girls' Brigade), and a couple of items from the junior section, a Christian Education item and a camp sketch. Looking at the preparations for the 1973 display these would occupy most evenings for the four weeks before the display with a full rehearsal the night before. Including the opening inspections, Captain's report and awards, the display would normally take two hours. The programme did vary year by year depending upon the Company strength. In some years there was no band item as in 1973 and 1976, in others no camp sketch (1971 and 1976).

The standard of the display was generally high as this note from Eric Jones, Captain of the 104th London and Inspecting Officer in 1976 wrote.

"We enjoyed very much seeing the 70th at work, and at home. We all believe very strongly in the purpose and method of the Boys' Brigade and I sincerely hope that this attitude is adopted by all the Boys, more especially the Senior ones, as well as the staff of course. I have seen the 70th at worship, and now at work. It is all good, and keen and very worthy of our organisation. You are to be congratulated. As regards the Display itself and the Boys, we enjoyed the Drill, the Final Item and the P.E. most of all. The Juniors were energetic and enthusiastic and the Safety First-Aid item showed us a great deal of what you did in the space of a few minutes. If I were a Boy in the Company I'd be looking at the Boys' Handbook very closely to see how to wear my uniform perfectly correctly, and what colour tie to wear on an important parade. I'd also be checking what badges I can get next year, and how I can aim at the highest Awards, like President's and Queen's if possible. I think I'd also make it as sure as possible that I got a Service Badge by being loyal to Bible Class and Drill almost every week. These are the things that make a B.B. Company strong, and I do congratulate the Boys who got Service Awards and the 100% Boy particularly. Those are the things I'd aim at and I hope you don't mind me mentioning them. But as for the spirit of the Company, the Display, the leadership and hope for your Seventieth year, you have every hope of a splendid anniversary, no trouble at all."

Despite the low staffing complement the company was still able to provide the boys both in winter and summer with a full programme of activities and with something on most nights of the week. Activities were moved around to fit the availability of staff with PT and Gym moving to a Saturday morning in 1974, and members of the Company joined the London Gym team taking part in the 1979 London District display. Greater use was made of Fridays with some badge work taking place in addition to drill and first aid which was also moved to that day. The 1974/5 annual report gives a flavour of life.

"The session (1974/5) found the company strength at 26. However, five of our senior boys found it impossible to remain in the company, which meant we started the session with one NCO and two other

Company Scenes from the 1970's

seniors. A revised programme of activity found us transferring First Aid to a Drill parade evening and PT and gym to a Saturday morning. The radical change brought an added interest to both classes. The crafts class, also working on a Friday evening, have evidence of their endeavour in the Display boards hanging in the B.B Room." Other activities were not forgotten "The month of January always finds the B.B Company preparing for annual competition, in our case amongst the companies in our battalion. This year we only entered the P.R.Games and came in third place, proving that being small is no real handicap."

The following year's report shows that the company was able to build on the previous year with slightly better numbers and more active involvement in battalion events

"The activities of the session have been reasonably well attended and have included PT and Gym -First Aid -Safety -Hobbies -Football - Table Tennis - Christian Education, apart from the regulation meetings of Drill and Bible Class. In the Battalion we have taken part in the Squad efficiency competition finishing in last place, though there were only a few marks separating the last four companies. P.T. Games competition was a little better with our team finishing sixth out of 13 teams. Football found us taking the runners up position, only dropping points to the league winners." These results may not sound particularly good but they should be taken in the context of an average size company with minimal staff in what was the largest battalion in London.

One activity, which was a precursor of things to come, was the company's first foray into the realms of the National competitions. In the early 1970's these were run under the auspices of the Stedfast Magazine, the magazine produced for boys in the Brigade. In the first year of entry in 1975/6 the company reached the third round before losing to a company from Weybridge. A few years later the company also tried its hand at volleyball in the national competition.

There were also significant changes to the fabric of the church in the 1970's which affected the company's operations. In 1973 the Main hall was converted into a new sanctuary for the church as the old church, built in 1908, was demolished. This loss of space would have significantly impeded the company when it was 50+ strong but was manageable with smaller numbers. However, the loss of the hall with its badminton court meant that the Old Boys Association felt that they could no longer undertake their main social activities, in particular badminton on a Monday night, and the Association closed in 1973. The Cricket club continued under the title of Seveno and still had Old Boys playing for it some 25 years later when they played a company team in 1998 as part of the Company's 90th anniversary celebrations. The loss of the Old Boys Association meant that unless a boy was in membership of the church at discharge at 18 there was no continuing direct linkage which with the steady stream of boys who reached the age limit from the late 1970's onwards would have been a positive benefit.

Throughout the 1970's the Junior Section was under the Leadership of George Bartlett meeting originally on a Friday before the Company section, before moving to a Monday in the late 1970's. The programme and activities remained similar to that of the Lifeboys of old and a steady stream of boys were promoted to the Company Section in September of each year. This extract from the 1975 report gives a flavour of a year's work. "During the summer we met as usual on Figges Marsh, this time is enjoyed by the boys and staff. We started off the session with 16 boys and as the session progressed our numbers have grown to 26. We welcomed Miss Olive Watson at the start of the session and she has been invaluable, operating the achievement award scheme. Many of the boys have gained their badges. Mr. Jim Ballard has also given us great service with our football team, we thank him for his efforts - our team finished in fourth position in the Battalion league. The section supper was quite good, whilst not so grand as the company, the sausage and mash seemed to go well, with not very much left anyway, our chaplain (Mr Reddaway) certainly liked the menu. Our thanks to all the parents who week by week send their sons to the halls on Friday evenings, thank you for your support. Here I would like to thank my staff Miss Olive Watson and Martin Richardson for the work they put in each Friday, and I emphasise this is every Friday, for we do not have long breaks. Thanks also to Mr.P.Knights and his staff for their support and help during the session. Once again we ask for the prayers of our church for all of us who serve the Lord, in serving in The Boys' Brigade."

Throughout the 1970's the pre-junior section or Blue Imps, met separately from the company on a Wednesday evening. Such groups became part of the Brigade officially as the Anchor boys in September 1977. This group served for the needs of boys aged 5 to 8 years. There was no badge or other arrangements for this group and the activities were largely fun based. As Prince Onyemachi, who joined the section in 1979 describes, "First Day-29th November 1979: Being brought into the church hall by my sister and my first activity was "what's the time Mrs Wolf"…Mrs Wolf was Elsa Hutchinson and along with Jim Ballard moulded so many of us the right way"

The Company section strength increased in both 1976 and 1977 and this increase in numbers and responsible senior boys led to a renewed confidence in the company. NCO's meetings that provided valuable feedback to the staff from the boys were restarted in 1976 for the first time since 1973, and some of the issues discussed such as dealing with lateness at Bible class were similar to those of earlier years. However, attendance levels were up and for instance at the October 1976 Founders Day Bible class 29 out of 30 boys were present. There was a general view that things were on the "up". This positive mood continued throughout 1977 and by 1978 for the seventieth year celebrations there was an optimistic note in Peter Knights annual report to the church meeting in February 1978.
"I am pleased to report that the Company, now entering its 70th Session of continuous activity is facing the difficulties of the age with an assured certainty. Those boys who are members have the freedom to terminate their membership when they wish, but facts speak for themselves, namely that with an average strength of B.B. company being approximately 20, the friendship and fellowship found among the members maintains a membership at fifty per cent above average. This provides the Company Staff and the supportive Church a real positive agency for the development of boys and to the attainment of the Object, with boys finding Jesus Christ as their own Saviour and Lord, becoming sound members of His Church. Let us take a glimpse at some details.

To be a member today is a privilege, for the heritage and past glories of the Company are a standard which are second to none and attainable only by the best. The membership today is as follows:-
Pre-Junior Section (The Imps) - 5, Junior Section - 20, Company Section - 32 .Staffed by 2 Lieutenants, 2 Warrant Officers and 3 other helpers who have particular responsibilities as P.T. Instructor, Football Manager and Pianist. During the summer session, former Captain Mr Bowbeer helped the Company as instructor of the Naturalists Badge Class, also serving Camp as Chaplain in the absence of a Pastor. The Pre-Junior Section (The Imps), from September 1st, 1977 became an integral part of the Boys' Brigade and our Company, a small unit at present, but a group for 6-8 year olds to enjoy and share together.

The Company activities play a very important part in the development of the boy and to this end encouragement in Athletics - Bugle Band - Communications - Camping- First Aid - Arts and Crafts - Naturalists - P.T. and Gym - swimming - Football - Cricket - Table Tennis - Scripture Knowledge - D of E Scheme - have all taken their respective place in both the work of the Company and the interest of the boy. Most of these activities comprise the current Company programme, with badges being earned and gained. This year we saw two of our boys gain the President's Badge, the previous holder of this award being Tony Foard who gained the award at its inception. The meetings of Drill Parade and Bible Class remain the obligatory twin pillars of the work in any Company. We still meet on Friday evenings and Sunday mornings with the Squad Medal Competition and Missionary Offering at Bible Class. In many ways the Company of yesterday is still the Company of today, the boys being different, the attitude being different, but one thing remains constant. They grow and develop into men and during the years that a boy is a member of the Company the object continues to be to introduce that boy to Christ, that he may know Him as Lord and that His Holy Spirit may change that boy into a Christian man. The implications that are before the Company are numerous, but I am sure that the "Situations Vacant" notice in God's Employment Bureau· will receive more than one enquiry to ensure that the work of this Company will continue. In this our 70th year we have set some targets that we may work toward, to improve our efficiency: as a

Company, an improved attendance record, at present running at 88 per cent; within our Battalion work, a striving toward a good position in the competitions of Drill and Scripture Knowledge, P.T. and Games, Gymnastics, Football and Table Tennis. We have been able to form two Football teams this year. Other particular events to mark this 70th year involve the Parents and Boys when we enjoyed an evening together at the annual social. The parents of boys play an important part in the life of the Company that an event shared together will give to us all a pleasure in being part of the 70th. The main event will be the 70th Annual Inspection and Display, which will include a reunion and parade of past members. The date will be Saturday 29th April, 1978."

The optimistic view of the Captain was surprisingly not born in total by the NCO's who expressed the view at a meeting with the officers that "drill and uniform standards are frequently poor. Apathetic

Company Section 1977

124

attitudes are common in Bible Class, especially regarding habitual lateness." The truth was probably a mix of the two as the following incident explains. The company for the first time in many years entered the two section drill competition. When the results were published despite being some 20 plus marks in front of the second company, the 70th were disqualified because they were two boys short of the required 26 boys. Stephen Ballard who was a boy in the company takes up the story. "When we got back to the church we were so angry. Without exception we all went round to see the two boys who had let us down by not coming and let them know in no uncertain terms what we thought of them."

The 70th year display saw a change of venue utilising the facilities at Eastfields School Mitcham rather than the Church halls, which were used earlier in the afternoon for a well attended former member's reunion, many of whom then attended the display in the evening. The display included a wide range of activities including both two section drill in pill boxes, a high quality box work item and a company band item. There was also a special guest item of a performance by an Old Boys band, many of whom had not played for many years.

The following day a joint parade was held to Longley Rd with the 37th and 47th London Companies who were according to the programme notes also sharing their seventieth anniversary. The parade service was taken by the then London Secretary Gerald Walker. However, there is no record in the London District records of the 47th being founded in 1908, as an earlier incarnation of a company with the same designation based in Walworth was already in being in that year, the 47th was in fact founded at Summerstown Mission in 1929.

The following year saw for no apparent reason a drop in numbers which was not offset by the company taking part in the nationwide publicity for the Brigade through the "First for Boys" campaign. The company put a significant amount of effort into this with local events but as with much of the brigade both within the battalion and nationally the end results were disappointing in terms of numbers recruited and retained.

70th Annual Inspection and Display,
held at Eastfields School -May 1978

Camp scenes early 1970's

At the start of the 1970's Camp was very much as it had been for the last two decades camping with the 3rd Sutton (Mid Surrey Company), in 1970 at Sidmouth, 1971 saw a return to the Isle of Wight at Whitecliff Bay and further new camp partners from 1st Whitstable, 15th Croydon and 1st Canterbury. A total of some 34 boys from the five Companies attended, with the 70th having the largest contingent of 12 boys but three staff, including Peter Knights and David Reddaway the chaplain. The camp prayers were based on the Journey into Life booklet. The following year there was a break with a number of camp traditions in that the company not only camped by itself for the first time but camped outside of the summer period using the May half term to camp at Whitchurch near Reading. Some 15 boys and six staff went on this camp which had two day trips out to Stratford and Windsor on the Tuesday and Thursday. There was also a bit of a lay- in with reveille slipping until 7.00am from the traditional 6.30am and Lights out at the latish hour of 10.20pm.

David Reddaway, who was Company Chaplain and attended many of the camps in this period fully entered into the spirit of Camp as Neil Pheasant recalls. "One notable enthusiast was David Reddaway, who was Pastor at TJBC during the early 70s. He was nicknamed "Rooster" by the boys, something to do with his stance when goalkeeping in the staff / boys football match. He was a great guy - even when some unnamed individuals filled his wellingtons with water and his sleeping bag with holly."
From 1973 to 1977 the 70th camped with the 118th London Company at various sites in the East Sussex Area. These were traditional camps even down to the menu which despite the growing racial mix within the company included largely traditional English fare such as steak and kidney pie, stewed steak and dumplings and roast lamb, plum duff was only served the once. Prayers were led by the chaplain or chaplains if in camp or at other times by the officers themselves as in 1977 when the outlines were prepared by Arthur Bowbeer who came to camp as chaplain in the absence of a "reverend". In that particular week the talks were based around the "Evangelism Explosion" teaching method, something that had been recently introduced to the church at Tooting. One member of the company who was present at that camp, Carl Osborne, remembered

the questions when writing some 20 years later "One of the most vivid memories I have is of my first BB Camp at Ashburnham, Sussex in 77. The Camp Padre, Arthur Bowbeer asked us two questions: -1. If you were to die tonight, would you go to heaven or hell? 2. If you were standing before God and He was to say to you, why should I let you into my Heaven? What would you say?

I was very worried, as I didn't know the answers. It did, however, start a search for faith that resulted in my trusting Christ some months later."

After 1977, possibly in response to comments made by the NCO's after the 1977 camp, a fresh look was taken at options for camping in the Company's seventieth year.

Camp in 1978 took the form not of a static camp but was programmed as a lightweight tour around a number of former sites in the Dorset and Devon area. The route and sites were meticulously planned but no amount of planning can account for the vagaries of the English weather. The group of 11 boys and 3 staff set out on the Friday evening by Minibus and set up camp outside Ringwood, moving to Swanage on the Saturday morning after each group cooked their own breakfast. So far so good until the rain came on the Saturday evening remaining on and off until the camp was moved on the Monday to Chideock. By this time the site at Chideock was under water and the group drove back to Bridport "feeling wet and cold and somewhat disappointed". Accommodation was fixed up in Bridport church hall and "following a strange night sleeping in conditions that could best be described as a "do-it-yourself Sauna", we awoke to the usual rain which was causing a real effect of apprehension as to what we could do today." The following day was spent in Weymouth returning to Bridport, and getting a parking ticket and the Wednesday move to Sidmouth was cancelled because of bad weather. By the Thursday the tentage was dry enough to move back to Sidmouth before returning to Tooting. A grand tour of 525 miles but which had been largely spoiled as an event by the inclement weather.

In 1979 no formal camp was undertaken although a weekend away was held with the 99th London. For 1980,this was Peter Knight's last camp as Captain, as earlier in April 1980 he had written to the church as follows.

"Throughout the past session, I have been deeply concerned as Captain, as to my ability to manage and lead the Company forward, in an imaginative and enthusiastic manner into the 1980s. Through many ways I have found that the necessary drive and energy to motivate others has been lacking in varying degrees, relying more on the initiative and sense of leadership of my brother officers and N.C.Os.

In my report to the church meeting in February, I mentioned the question of adequacy of leadership and the need to solve this problem as a necessity toward progress. Toward that solution, I believe that at this point in time the Company should have a new leader, a person that will be able to motivate and draw the tremendous resources of talent which are available, but dormant, among the staff and members today.

Recent pressures of business and health have tended to lay in my thinking, facts which cannot be totally ignored. I believe that in some way the Lord has been saying, perhaps for some time, lay down this work, it is for another to lead on. It is therefore after much prayer and consideration that I have taken the decision to resign my membership of the 70th.London Company, and in particular as Officer and Captain. The Company is the responsibility of the Church. I would however leave before you for your deliberations, my lieutenant Neil Pheasant. Neil supported me with the Company over the past seven years. The effect of the change would be at the close of the current session on 31st August 1980."

The church accepted Peter's recommendation and Neil became the 70th's fifth Captain in September 1980. It is fair to say that without Peter's efforts in the 1970's that the Company could well have closed. After 1980 Peter remained active in Brigade work becoming initially a Battalion Vice President and then Battalion Secretary, also assisting the company whenever possible.

First For Boys Campaign 1979/80

The early eighties-1980-84

Neil Pheasant started as the 70th's fifth Company Captain in a situation totally different to any of his predecessors without the numbers of staff and boys that Peter Knights and Arthur Bowbeer had or the staff number, albeit inexperienced, that Bert Porter or William Cotsell had. Neil's one lieutenant was George Bartlett who was running the Junior Section with Jim Ballard, who was completing officers training. However what Neil did have was enthusiasm and a good group of senior NCO's.

Writing in 1988 about the handover Neil comments "It was very much the end of an era when, in 1980, Peter Knights gave up the reins of the Captaincy he had held since 1961. The thought for me of the 70th without 'Curly', as the Boys (and Staff) called him, was not easy to imagine. However, although the number of Boys was only 14, the Company's foundations were as strong as ever.

My first Drill Parade as the new 'Skipper' fell on the night before my wedding in October 1980. (My wedding suit was, coincidentally, just the right colour and style for BB uniform). I was in much fear and trembling, and felt the Boys watching my every move for some mistake or missing point of detail. I was the only Company Section Officer and am more conscious in hindsight of the enormity of the task than I ever was at the time. But God was gracious and provided the necessary assistance in George Bartlett and Jim Ballard from the Junior Section, and Keith Sylvester, new to B.B. work. Others led badge classes and we were blessed by good, faithful, Christian NCO.s - what more can a Captain want or need? Sadly, Keith married and emigrated to New Zealand in 1982".
Keith has the distinction of being the first non-white officer in the Company.
"My new NCO's were Steve Ballard, Philip Charles, Paul Parker and Carl Osborne - a great team. We worked hard to get things "right", building on the traditional foundations of Bible Class and Drill Parade - and introducing a programme of other activities that had us meeting every day of the week at times. The previous years had been challenging, and many wondered if the BB was still a useful evangelistic tool for the churches. We knew they were wrong. My

big concern was Bible Class. The object of the BB is "The advancement of Christ's Kingdom amongst Boys ...." Trusting that God would bless us if we put that first we were encouraged to see the Company grow, and some go on to follow Christ. Boys just HAD to be there. If they did not hear the Christian message then, whatever else we might do to serve them, the most important thing would be missing."

Neil goes on to write "Keith was soon replaced by Chris Buss, an enthusiastic ex-Boy and Officer from the 79th London (East Hill Wandsworth) who provided much needed experience. The Boys too were an enthusiastic lot and hitherto esoteric subjects like Heraldry gained in popularity. We entered Competitions with more optimism than skill and were rewarded in February '82 with the Battalion P.R .games Trophy - the first cup for 15 years. I seem to remember a celebration in McDonalds at Balham afterwards, with some very wary looks from other customers. Successes in Vaulting, Groundwork etc soon followed."

By the early 1980's the Wandsworth battalion was no longer the largest battalion with regards to boy membership in London but was still in the top three. However, within the area attitudes to the Brigade within churches were changing and at least two strong companies (those at Southfields and Mitcham Lane Baptist) were closed because the church no longer felt that the Brigade was the right form of outreach for them. Despite these closures the winning of any battalion event still had a sense of achievement particularly for what was in effect a small company against the larger companies such as the 88th and 181st who had had virtually a duopoly on battalion competitions for most of the past decade.

During the early 1980's, despite continuing low staff levels, the company maintained an active weekly programme including running a Saturday football team and regular summer badge activities such as craft, expedition and naturalist badges. Bible Class and drill were still the mainstay of the Company and Bible Class was led mainly by the staff with far fewer outside speakers. This was due to a number of factors such as the lower number of companies and many companies merging Bible class with other Sunday church activity. This general decline in Bible Class activity is best reflected in the fact that in the mid 1980's the Brigade stopped publishing an annual Bible class handbook and this in itself made the organisation of Bible Class more difficult as the staff had to use other resources than the handbook. In truth for a few years some of the better annual syllabuses or sections from them were recycled together with other material from Scripture Union and other sources. However, speakers were by largely restricted to the company staff.

The Company display also took on a new lease of life under Neil's captaincy. The first display in 1981 had a definite theme similar to that of the 1950's with a Star Wars theme. This included the use of ultra violet lights, light sabres etc., all in the church hall, with a much reduced space available for performance. Other items included as in days of old camp sketch, drill and gym, with items from the Juniors and Anchor boys.

Company badge work had items such as expedition and first aid but also included computers with the company investing in the latest high tech. computers, a Sinclair ZX81 and then a ZX spectrum. How much time was spent on programming them was debatable - a lot more time was spent by boys and staff playing space invaders!

1983 saw the centenary of the Brigade and the Company's 75th anniversary. During the centenary year there were a number of special events and the District cancelled all competitions so that a special emphasis could be made on the Centenary. These celebrations saw the Company back at the Royal Albert Hall playing a major part in the Battalion item which was a re-creation of the 1943 Windsor Castle review. This meant many practice sessions and dusting down and cleaning pillboxes, which fitted awkwardly on certain afro hair cuts, as members of the company formed either the inspection squad or a dummy brass band to be inspected once again by King George VI and the Royal Family. The four appearances at the Albert Hall gave boys a good view of the wider brigade in London and a taste of what could be done outside of the company. Every member of the company section took part in the display item.

The company display in 1983 was a reflection of past life in the

Company Scenes early 1980

Uniform Cleaning and Drill.

company including drill with rifles, a war based first aid item and 1950's P.T. exercises as well as box and mat work.

Royal Albert Hall 1983

Another part of the Centenary celebrations was a Royal review at Holyrood House, Edinburgh. The Company sent two NCO's, Phillip Charles and Carl Osborne, as well as the Company Captain to this event. There were also local Battalion superteam events on Tooting common, and a district Centenary day in Barnet in both of which the Company participated. The year concluded with a 75th anniversary Old Boys reunion with many old, and not so old, former members attending. Earlier in the year the battalion had paraded to the church, the drop in numbers of boy was noticeable when compared to earlier years. The centenary year also saw George Bartlett's retirement as officer in charge of the Junior Section and he was succeeded by Jim Ballard.

1983 also saw a change to the company section badge structure. The 20 or so barrel shaped individual subject badges introduced in 1968, and reduced to plastic in the mid 1970's, were swept away with five new badges that covered a variety of topics under the headings of Leadership, Adventure, Physical, Community and Interests. There were three stages for each one. If you achieved all five at level three then the President's Badge was earned. Individual subject credits were gained and a sticker was earned and recorded in the boy's handbook. One side product of the new badge system was that when it came to the display, the time taken to announce the awards handed out to some boys went on and on and on .

The centenary also saw the phasing out of a piece of officer's uniform that was formerly carried by all officers and then just the captain - the walking stick. However, Neil Pheasant's walking stick vanished mysteriously before it could retire, somehow finding its way back to him as part of his retirement presentation.

One particular activity of note in Centenary year was the battalion fund raising effort which saw the Junior section boys and supporters walk up to ten laps of Figges Marsh, a total of ten miles, over £200 was raised by the 70th alone for the children's ward at St.Georges Hospital .

The Company numbers were not sufficient to consider a feasible company camp and in 1981 the 70th resumed its long association with the 37th London and camped with them at Sidmouth, together with the 47th London and the 2nd Herne Bay. Normal service was resumed with the NCO's playing the normal pranks on the staff, although Paul Parker was somewhat surprised that a certain member of staff noticed that the camp flag pole had been removed from outside the marquee and inserted into his sleeping bag. The 70th continued to camp with this group throughout the 1980's and in doing so became acquainted with the 37th medical officer one Brian Prichard - a name that would become legendary over the next twenty years to 70th boys at camp for his driving skills, pilchard sandwiches and camp walks amongst other things. One walk of particular note at the 1982 camp at Ilfracombe involved a misjudged tide and smaller boys carried on staff and seniors shoulders to avoid the need for full clothed swimming. The 1984 camp walk at Porlock, near Minehead, involved a walk up a goat track that the goats refused to go up and a 70 degree climb up the side of the cliff.

The camp in Centenary year was at Sidmouth and on a site that was adjacent to both a Girl's Brigade site and a donkey sanctuary. The latter was occasionally noisy but the former was of more interest to the senior boys and this interest led unfortunately after lights out to a day time visitation from the staff of the GB who camp who appeared to have no visible means of perambulation, and were thus unfortunately titled the "Castors" as they menacingly approached the camp. The Castors eventually left site after CO Dave Blake had advised them that the boy's intentions were strictly honourable.

After the Centenary session increased work commitments and ill health forced Neil to resign as Captain, and he was replaced in April 1984 by Chris Buss. Neil remained as an officer until 1988 when he went into the ministry, but his short but eventful Captaincy had laid good foundations for the future of the Company.

Late Nineteen eighties 1984-89

The Company in 1984 was in good heart despite numbers being at a low number when compared with the past, and being lower than the average sized company in the London or Wandsworth area. However, what the company lacked in quantity it made up in quality, sheer hard work and enthusiasm. This was evident in the showing at the Battalion athletics in 1984 when the company turned up with 13 boys, just sufficient to enter every event over the three age groups, and one, the overall event, without winning an individual event. The margin of victory was narrow, just four points, but it showed the boys what could be done against larger numbers if everyone took part even doing events they didn't fancy. The look on the faces of the other companies was worth seeing as the long wait for the Athletics trophy to come back to the 70th was ended. Winning the Athletics trophy marked the start of five years up until 1989 where the company won a large number of battalion events when there were still a good number of companies to compete against. Events won included competitions that the 70th had had a history in, such as vaulting, groundwork, cricket and athletics, but also included other events such as football, swimming and drill in which the company had had limited success in the past.

The Company, despite limited staff numbers, carried out a full programme. In addition to the staple diet of drill and Bible Class, the midweek programme included gymnastics, badge work and Band.

An account of life in the Company in the late 1980's follows from Vusi Siphika.
"I went along to the 70th in September 1985. As a new boy I entered the target squad, which gives a good insight and understanding into the workings and operations of the BB. We had to learn the history of the Brigade, the object, motto, drill and a basic understanding of the Christian Faith. Within the target squad it was instilled into us that we had to work hard for our badges. From this healthy competition with the other target squad lads occurred where we wanted to have good attendance, clean uniforms and to do well in drill. The squad system ensured new boys formed an integral part of the company. Here we were put under the control of a squad commander,

usually a NCO who would keep an eye on us. The NCO's set high standards and gave a positive example, making a new recruit think, 'Yes, I want to be like that'.

Friday night was the big night with drill parade. Drill could be off-putting for the newcomer with Mr Buss's voice raised to extremes that had the whole of Longley Rd quivering in their boots. Along with Mr Pheasant's bad jokes we were onto a winning combination. Drill would be followed by clubroom, which consisted of snooker, table tennis, football and board games. The other important meeting was Bible Class on a Sunday morning. To me Bible Class brought a sense of fellowship and brought everything together. If you like, a sense of bringing all the fun and good things we did in the Brigade and bringing them to God. Furthermore Bible Class provoked and challenged boys to decide which path they should follow - the path with Jesus Christ or the path without.

So what were some of the fun filled action packed sports activities, events and competitions and memorable moments that took place in my time in the 70th. Sport featured heavily with 11 a side football on Tooting Bec Common featuring some close encounters with the likes of the 37th. The Battalion under 14 five a side football was won at Spencer Park school. In other spheres the Company also flourished with a host of activities going on. The Duke of Edinburgh's award saw boys achieving Bronze and Silver, while various badge credits were earned in citizenship, first aid, fire prevention and expedition, to name just a few activities."

The Band briefly flourished again for five or so years between 1984 and 1989 competing and winning the battalion bugle team and taking part in the London competition, and even on one occasion leading the company in a pre-church parade, marching around the streets. But the difficulties in getting the boys to the practice venue based over in Wandsworth meant that it eventually "died" again in 1989.

Company numbers picked up over the late 1980's and settled around the mid twenties for most of the period. Attendance levels were also good and thus during 1985/86 the company won for only the second time in it's history the battalion efficiency competition.

Coincidentally the Colour was presented at the display when the inspecting officer was Les Wright who was in the company when the 70th were awarded the Colour in 1944. This increase in numbers in

the company and a healthy increase in juniors meant that with three officers something had to go, as there were insufficient staff to deal with Anchors, Juniors, Company and Senior boys. In the minds of the staff, work with the company age and senior boys was of greater import and the decision was made to cease the anchors boys in 1985. This was against the trend in Brigade work nationally where the tendency was for more work with the lower age range. In hindsight the move was correct as over the next twenty years the 70th maintained a relatively high number of senior (15+) boys.

In the following session, 1985/86 the Company won its first two London District trophies for almost twenty years. The first of these was the Physical recreation Games trophy, whilst the second was a tie with the 3rd Enfield in the 11-a- side Cricket. The final few overs of this match saw the 70th batting in ever decreasing gloom so that the batsmen were literally batting by street light, but fortunately we scraped home the required number of runs despite the darkness. This tie led to a remarkable sequence in this competition with the 70th being runners up in the next two years to the 3rd Enfield and then winning every year until 1995 and being either winner or runner up until the competition ceased in 1999. The 70th bowling attack, particularly in the late 1980's, had little room for guile being largely based on sheer pace. In one memorable London game the 13th Bromley were bowled out for 13 and then our own batsmen collapsed to 0-4, with the team captain, Arthur Howell, striding back after his duck with the immortal words "Watch out Lads, they are bowling straight." The team scraped the remaining runs with the loss of only one more wicket.

In addition to the eleven-a-side game the Company also had success in the six-a-side game which required a degree of balance, as the team needed five competent bowlers who could also bat. After an initial foray in 1986, the 70th won the district trophy in 1987, were disqualified for lateness in 1988 and then won again in 1989. Perhaps one of the most memorable shots of all these competitions was when Chris Howell almost disembowelled the square leg umpire as he square cut a ball for six with what appeared to be the minimum of effort.

The Company also re-entered the London Gym competition at the same time and suddenly found a use for a strange piece of redundant gym equipment which no-one has seen in use for a few years, or knew its purpose, the parallel bars. Having seen them in use whilst waiting to take part in the London vaulting and groundwork events, the boys largely self taught then went on to not only take part in the competition, to win it for the next three years, but also to perform an item in the 1988 London Display.

The company also had a good record in drill in the late 1980's; under the tuition of Neil Pheasant the company twice reached the London finals finishing third both times. The finals were held at Parsons Green, the National and London Brigade HQ, which had been purchased with much effort from the Brigade membership in the 1960's only to be sold in 1988. A sign perhaps that the Brigade nationally was in decline.

The Company section success in competitions also spread to the Juniors as Prince Onyemachi describes:

"After winning every trophy there was to win at Junior section level in 1985 we were fortunate enough to be allowed to take the trophies into school and then we had to stand up and be applauded - a dozen of us from different years all very proud to have achieved the treble". The section had come a long way in three years as Prince also describes "My First tournament - 1982/3: Handball tournament played at Welham Road church hall, only 3 turned up for the 5-a-side and we made a team along with a couple from the 118th, and got very well beaten that day, but it was the start of many a tournament adventure"

Mining the competitive streak within the boys was only a means to an end, as Andrew Johnson wrote back in 1988.

"There was never a dull moment in the Brigade: from swimming to squad drill, cricket to chess, and band to badminton. I was promoted early in the second year and this heralded something that goes hand in hand with progression through the Brigade - Responsibility.

We entered competitions and grew from the level of hoping to win, to expecting to win ...... and went to Scotland for the all Finals..

At this time I thought going to Church and having a Bible in my room would get me to Heaven. The Brigade was about to prove me wrong. We went to Camp and there Christ suddenly and wonderfully questioned me, but believing I was a Christian already gave me an excuse to forget it. Then I went to a Christian leadership weekend at Elm Tree farm and Christ asked me to make a concrete commitment to Him. I got baptised a few months later The Brigade clearly shows that Christ - not the competitions - is the important thing. My greatest moment was when Cpl Barrington Green and I were the Brigade representatives at an event for organisations involved in the Duke of Edinburgh's Award Scheme and the Duke chatted to me and cracked jokes."

Andrew's reference to the Duke of Edinburgh's award shows that the Company was still actively involved in this programme. One of the autumn expeditions which Andrew was involved in had the misfortune to forget to take the batteries for the torch, thus spending twelve hours plus of darkness in their two man tents whilst a couple of years later nature also took an active part in rerouting an expedition as Prince Onyemachi describes. "My sister managed to get to Silver DofE (which looks much nicer than the Bronze which I got too), but one of the accomplishments that most sticks in my mind as a boy in the company is when we planned to do the walk, and then the great winds happened and the paths that we tried to follow were covered in trees that had fallen over, so we made an alternative route"

The Company displays of the late 1980's were in the best tradition of BB displays, literally a presentation of the work of the Company over the previous twelve months. Unlike the earlier displays the presence of newer technologies allowed both the use of lights, flashes and actions but also for the activities to be videoed for future posterity.

It seems that each display had at least one "special" item which was out of the ordinary,
including the formation of the 1st Covent Garden Company with drill as art, or was it ballet; the BB in 2000BC (not sure how that ties into the object!!) but the boys looked interesting in the animal skin sacks or the recreation of the Royal Tournament cannon run complete with our own firing cannon with smoke. The displays were also well supported by both Church and Parents. In addition to the special items there were also the regular events such as best drilled private and the award of the Esprit de Corps cup, as Prince Onyemachi again describes: "In the Best Drilled Private1987- I wish I hadn't turned right when the others in the squad turned left! I remember asking a man in the front row to 'Please tell me that they are all wrong and that I'm right and have won' … he just shook his head, whilst I was asked to join the rest of the squad…nice. I managed to win the Esprit de Corps trophy twice and as it was voted for by your peers it was one of the most valuable things a boy could win….not to mention the free trip to camp that accompanied the trophy which always came in handy."
The Company's 80th year in 1988 saw the display move from the church hall to the hall at Graveney School (Formerly Rosa Bassett School), and involved in one form or another five of the Company's six Captains. The previous week a dozen or so Old Boys met in the church hall to practice as a band. At the display it's fair to say they stole the show with drum major Brian Rance leading them in as if it was Buckingham Palace and 1951 all over again. Later that year the Company again held a successful reunion of former members.
In addition to local and London events the company also started to take a closer interest in the national competitions. These were initially run under the auspices of the Stedfast magazine, which was published for boy members of the brigade, but were now run by BB HQ. In the mid 1980's there were five events - five-a-side football,

chess, table tennis, Top of the form and volleyball. It was the latter that the 70th developed a particular skill in, despite the confines of practicing in a low-ceilinged church hall with the attendant risk of being hit by a dislodged fluorescent tube. The company entered the event and reached the United Kingdom finals in 1986. These were held in Paisley outside Glasgow and the boys and staff were hospitably received by the parents of the Paisley lads who hosted our team in their homes. We were beaten in the semi final by the Northern Irish team - 1st Knocknamuckley with whom we would have much contact over the coming years, but in overall terms it was a very positive experience that led on to the next twenty years of positive engagement with these competitions.

In the following year we again took part in the Finals that were part of the All finals days held in Falkirk although we qualified as a lucky loser having been beaten by the 32nd Cardiff in the semi final who then had to pull out of the final. We also played Cardiff in the Albert Hall, as both companies took part in the last ever London display at the Royal Albert Hall in May 1987 in a demonstration volleyball game that was played with vigour and competitive edge. That year's display had a range of interesting and unusual items including immediately after the volleyball a steel band item by another local company the 104th London. We met the Cardiff boys two years later in the 1989 finals which they hosted a day which is best remembered for the events at Hillsborough in Sheffield.

Between the two meetings with Cardiff the company also reached the finals of the Volleyball in 1988. These were held in Motherwell, and after the event the Company had one of its more nerve wracking experiences on a trip to the local chippie. An everyday experience in most towns, but the sight of a dozen or so black youngsters in this particular Scottish town brought the noisy local residents out of the local hostelries, who were not used to such sights, with the result that the local constabulary gave us a police escort back to the church hall we were staying in, for safe keeping until we caught the midnight train back to Euston

One of the company's more memorable events in the National competitions was the National five-a-side Football trip to Colchester

Company Gym item and Old Boys Band from
the 80th Company Display May 1988.

where in no particular order we managed to wrench off the fuel cap of the hired minibus, then wedge the minibus into the entrance of a multi storey car park and leave one boy hospitalised after an argument with the wall of the local leisure centre. That was one argument that Andrew Johnson lost but unfortunately the team was knocked out as well as him.

The company also had a degree of success in the more cerebral of competitions and in 1987 reached the semi final of the Chess competition loosing to the overall winners of the UK event the 2nd Hythe 5-3. The following year the 70th reached three out of the five UK finals of volleyball as previously mentioned, five-a-side football and table tennis. For the latter we travelled to West Bromwich and we again had the misfortune to draw the eventual winners from Edinburgh losing 5-2. We were also close to the final in table tennis in the following two years, losing both times to a Lowestoft company who had two Chinese lads one of whom had the scariest serve ever seen.

London Display 1987 and 1988

These escapades to most parts of England as well as Scotland and Wales were enjoyed by both staff and senior boys alike and without question the hospitality of the host company were in the best BB traditions. The company's relative success and profile in terms of ethnicity also meant that we were called upon to take part in events that perhaps in the past would have gone to others. One such event was the opening of the new BB HQ in Hammersmith by HRH Prince Edward in 1988/89. The 70th provided not only staff and boys for the guard of honour but a select group of five boys to be interviewed inside by the Prince where they discussed what they had done in the Brigade to earn their Duke of Edinburgh's Award .In addition to these events of national importance the company also played a role with members of the 88th and 181st London, in making a short five minute film to be shown on the BBC. This took a lot longer to film than five minutes and involved Jimmy Hill on Clapham Common. This filming was fun to watch, even if it was perishing cold. The funniest bits didn't reach the TV screen as said Mr Hill was clattered by a few of the lads. Despite the impression shown above, the 70th's eleven-a-side football skills were actually improving and the main battalion eleven-a-side trophy was won for the first time in 1985 and then again in 1987. Home games had moved from Figges Marsh to Tooting Common as the pitches there were closed down by Merton Council. The 70th also provided over half the battalion team that won the London Competition in 1987. The Company also provided most of the boys for the athletics team that won the London event in 1986 and 1987, whilst at the same time being battalion champions throughout this period.

Despite the increase in time spent on competition events, the company still undertook the traditional pattern of events in the 1980's that earlier generations would have recognized whether it be the weekly routine or the annual cycle including events such as BB week, Christmas Carol singing, Company supper, Display and then Camp. As referred to earlier the 70th had reverted to camping with the 37th and in the mid to late 1980's the Camps changed from the 70th being the minor partner to becoming a major partner. Between 1985 and 1987 Camp was in Devon at Ilfracombe, Sidmouth and Salcombe respectively and in both 1988 and 1989 the Isle of Wight was visited. Each of these camps had its own story and tales to tell. Sidmouth in 1986 was notable for the rain at least four consecutive days of it and a low cloud that meant that the end of the camp square couldn't be seen from the Marquee. It was also the last year that part of the canvas was bell tents. For a number of years 14 foot ridges had crept into the camp canvas and had gradually edged out bell tents. Sidmouth was the last year we used bell tents and it was the year that the bells caused more problems weather wise than the ridges. The following year at Salcombe was perhaps the most memorable of those camps starting at the beginning with the camp field being split in two; the incident of the advance guard lorry getting lost, damaging local drainage ditches and then itself having the back almost ripped off as the driver misjudged the way into and out of the camp field. On the way home as Neil Pheasant recalls "The MO gave me some painkillers that sent me to sleep - beside a field somewhere near Exeter with a bus load of boys milling around and wondering what to do as the muck-spreaders approached - on an extremely hot summer's afternoon!. I can still smell the smell and hear the exclamations". In spite of, or because of these privations, the camp was one of the most successful of modern times, in particular in a spiritual sense.

These camps with three companies of similar camp strengths and a shared outlook were camps where there was keen rivalry between the companies in tent competition. It was not unknown for a tent on their day off of tent inspection, as they were the orderly tent, to try and get the tent inspection done before orderlies at 7.00am. This often involved illicit work before reveille at 6.30am but the motives were genuine in trying to be the best . This competitive edge also included camp sports which were organized on a tent basis covering the evening period after tea, with the tents taking part in volleyball, football and non stop cricket. The boys also played the staff at these three events and some of the tackling in the football was literally bone crunching, with little quarter given or asked for on both sides.

A general view of late 1980's camps is given by Vusi Siphika. "To me the work and events of my life in the 70th can be summed up in the annual camps. Mr Buss organised, no expense spared, luxury camps in exotic locations such as Devon, Isle of Wight and Swanage. Grass fields, tents, cold water washing, The Prof's walks through the bush, and sports always made for a memorable camp. In particular I found camps interesting when there were neighbouring camps. The sight of collapsed tents in their fields always bemused me. How could they have got like that? However the ultimate experience of Camp and the BB is the sense of fellowship and closeness with our Saviour Jesus Christ. An experience that will never change from generation to generation" Prince Onyemachi, a contemporary, writes "Showers, What showers? Bathing in cold water out in the middle of a field at 6am was an experience that the youngsters these days wouldn't believe if they were told about it, but I'm glad I was part of the old school as I was given the old school values that served the company so well in the past...

Docs walk: In the mid 80's it was advisable to carry a machete with you if you didn't have a medical reason why you couldn't do the monstrosity of a walk, as the terrain would be quite fierce. 1986 was a brilliant year for the walk as we had to stop ourselves falling down a steep hill by grabbing onto trees that were sprouted out of inclines in the ground. The walks toned down over the years, but the simple mention of "Docs Walk" used to scare the most ardent camper. What a way to walk off the Plum Duff.

Plum Duff: Not sure who invented it, but my goodness, it was almost as good as Andrew Thomas's mum's cakes... almost being the word as she was a master cake chef and it wasn't until you had tasted the latter that you realised why they were reserved for "officers only"

Nigh time Activity: Everyone was supposed to stay in their tent, but it very rarely happened that way. There is really no experience like having a Commanding Officer stand on your back as you try to explain why you have come out of the wrong side of the tent to where the latrines were. A big thank you goes to Freddie Adu / Peter Williams / Andrew "Ninja Man" Thomas, for a momentous night which culminated in Mr Buss being woken by the leaders of a neighbouring campsite, who, after frog marching me down the hill, asked Mr Buss "Is this Yours ?"....I'd never been referred to as "This" before or since..."

The boys were not the only people to get up to tricks at camp at the 1989 camp. It was noted that one of our regular staff members, one of the 37th officers, had "deserted" to a beach mission. So an elaborate kidnap attempt was organized. The offending member of staff was spotted on an afternoon off with other members of the beach Mission staff playing crazy golf. A few minutes later the camp transit van pulled up, the Sinclair brothers ran out the back, literally kidnapped the member of staff concerned straight into the back of the van which drove off at high speed. The confused member of staff

Battalion Athletics 1988- Tooting Bec Track
Camp Church parade -Salcombe 1987

was driven around town until dropped off at the local railway station.

The two camps to the Isle of Wight in 1988 and 1989 marked the start of a trend in a change in camp activities. Traditionally most activities had taken place on the Camp site with off site activities being restricted to free day, swimming parades, church parade and the cross country. The availability of transport in the form of minibuses meant that it was possible to move to off site activities whether it be ten pin bowling, visits to places of interest or leisure activities such as Blackgang Chine. In addition, other activities such as the walk could start and finish at other places than the camp site. These additional activities meant that boys could be engaged without having an eye on them all the time in the camp field. At both of these camps we were visited by Gordon Wooderson who was ex-Captain of the 88th London and had a connection going back to the early 1920's when he was the inspecting officer at one of the Stubbington Camps as well as being a regular Bible Class speaker. Gordon spoke at the church parade for the 1989 camp which had a dual notability in that it was the last time the Company bugle band openly paraded and the last time he addressed the 70th. In many ways both marked the passing of an era for the Brigade as a whole and the 70th in particular. The world around was changing and locally companies were closing not only through lack of numbers but also again because of decisions being made by churches that the BB method wasn't suitable for them, so current and past camping partners such as the 37th and 181st disappeared into history and in ten years the local battalion had halved in size. The 70th had however doubled in strength over the decade and looked forward to the 1990's with confidence and anticipation.

The Nineties 1990-1999

At the start of 1990 the company in terms of competition success was on a high being London District Champions in four events and battalion champions in ten events. However, things with regard to the battalion were due to change. The strength of the battalion was down to 12 companies with an average company and senior section strength of 11 boys. The 70th's boy strength was 24 in the company and senior section and 15 juniors. The smaller size of the battalion meant that competitions were restricted to sporting events such as five a side football, swimming and athletics -the latter being held with Kingston and Merton, together with the scripture competition. The company also had a degree of national celebrity being one of the first companies featured in what was to be a regular item in the BB Gazette the "Company spotlight". The company had only two staff at Lieutenant rank Chris Buss as Captain and Jim Ballard being joined later in the decade by Barry Green who was promoted from warrant officer.

The absence of battalion events meant that the company had to look elsewhere for what in earlier days would have been routine activities such as football on a Saturday. With no other companies able or wiling to field an 11 a side team in the battalion over the decade the company took part in a range of activities. Initially organising a league that covered companies from South London . This lasted one season but fell through after that probably because the league was one sided .One game was won 30-0. After that football involved three seasons travelling to West Kent on a Saturday morning with both junior and company boys, then a season 1995-96 with two teams in the Association of combined youth clubs Saturday afternoon league, followed by a season of friendlies and then three seasons travelling to West London for games at junior and under 15 level. The company had a degree of success in these endeavours but the toll on the staff in travelling couldn't be counted.

The regular playing of 11 aside football meant that the company was able to provide the majority of the boys for the battalion team that took part District 11 a side football competition, winning this event on six occasions in the ten years 1991,92,93,95,98,99. The last two times with the whole squad being 100% made up of 70th boys. The first of these finals saw what in any generation was a significant sporting gesture in a game that was referred by a top division referee -Alf Buksh, the battalion gained a penalty .The boy who was allegedly fouled - Paul Mcintosh felt that it wasn't a foul so he took the penalty rolling the ball straight to the goalkeeper. His team mates may have had something to say about this if the result had turned out different to the 5-1 scoreline. The ability to provide regular football was both a good recruiting agent and retention method as these quotes demonstrate .Stephen Rock saying why he joined "I went there cause all my friend at the time were going there and were telling me about how good it was and the fact that they played a lots of different sports but mainly football." Nathan Asare adds "Initially it was the chance to play football every week. I think the reason I stayed is because I made a lot of good friends

The diminished size of the battalion meant that the battalion church parades, which had in earlier days seen 500+ boys marching down Church Lane having formed up on Tooting Bec Common were discontinued and replaced with a battalion bible class. At the one held at the 70th the speaker was Martin Bashir who held the boys attention well. Martin was also involved in the 70th's appearance on Songs of Praise as he was the presenter when the BBC did a programme on the BB which featured the 70th. The two and a half minutes that were actually shown took some four hours to film and included the company gym team, a "mock" Bible Class and the crime prevention class visiting a local police station. The final scene showed some of the boys inside a police cell as Vusi Siphika said "One image the programme left with me was of Wayne Henry locked in a police cell. What did he do wrong? We asked ourselves. Hadn't he attended a citizenship class!" The programme was shown in early 1991. Songs of Praise was not the only time that members of the 70th were before the camera as in 1992 members of the Junior section were filmed in a recruiting video for the junior section and a couple of years later company section members were also filmed.The use of the 70th boys added a splash of colour to casts that were otherwise rather pale!

Company Section
1976 above   1982 below

The Company Section
1991 above 2003 below

Camp Scenes from the 1970's

CAMP

1980

camp 1983 and 1987

Scenes from Camp 1989 and 1990

Camp 1991 and 1993

Camp 1995 and 1998

Camp 2002 and 2003

Company
Display

1981 and 1985

Company Display 1987

Company Display 1992 and 1993

Display 1995 & Junior Section

Expedition 1985

Royal Albert Hall 1987

With HRH Prince Edward At Opening of
New Brigade House in 1988,

Viscount Thurso, Brigade President in
Tooting in December 1988.

Eight 70th boys at the Royal review at Windsor
Castle in 1994

Senior boys acting as Stewards in 1995

Daily Telegraph Shield Winners

2003, and 2004

Daily Telegraph shield winners for the
third time in 2005. Ronald Frank and Ben
Lettman with HRH Duchess of Gloucester

UK National five a side winning teams
1993 above 1997 below

UK National five a side winning teams
2001 above
below Under 14 team 2003

Wandsworth Youth group of the year in 2004 Joint with
7th London GB and 2007

Table Tennis 1988

National
Finalists

Badminton
1998

Athletics 2006

Founder's day service St.Paul's Cathedral 1996

Stewards
1997

Above
1998

London
District
Junior
Section
Football
Side

2000
London
District
Athletics

London District Cross Country 2005

England And Wales under 14 and Under 18
Football 2007

Kool Drummings -Notting Hill 1998

Brigade Council, Dartford 1998

Kool Drummings on the Thames 2002
With Ainsley Harriott 2004

Kool Drummings appearing at the Baptist World Congress at the Birmingham NEC in July 2005.

Kool Drummings 1996 with HRH Prince of Wales

Double Take-Monopoly tour
of London 1996 and 2000

Former Members Reunions 1988 and 2005

Mid
week Camp
New Forest

2005

Visiting Belfast 2006 (above)

Edinburgh 2008 (Below)

A typical company programme during the early 1990's is as set out in the first edition of the company newsletter -"70 up" in September 1994.

Sunday Bible Class - 10.00am ;
Mondays Steel band 7.00pm;
Tuesdays Badminton 7.00pm,
Wednesdays Junior section 6.30pm ; Gym and Physical recreation 8.00 pm;
Fridays- Company Section 6.30pm ;Seniors 7.45pm;
Saturdays - Events as announced.

Effectively this was still a full weekly programme with the seniors reverting to their own programme on a Friday ; this became more distinct as the decade moved on. Drill still played a part on a Friday night although no longer the sole activity as parts of the evening were also given over to badge work and clubroom. For one session drill was taken by one of the boys parents who obtained a good standard of drill but his efforts were not particularly appreciated as Nathan Asare says "I hated drill I would try to get there late, so I would miss most of it".

Traditional events included the Company supper with food, fun and games at Christmas but in the 1990's it also included the showing of the previous years camp video filmed by Prof Prichard reminding boys of the previous year's camp and giving new recruits a glimpse of what they could look forward to.

The company display was still well attended and taking the 1992 display would have included a couple of junior section items, a safety sketch, a camp item and a comedy item.That year it was a drill parade from the future with the NCOs taking the roll on key boards , mat work, boxwork ,drill , parallel bars and a spiritual item . The first item was the Best Drilled Private competition and the last the presentation of awards. However the announcements of these when combined to the length of badge credits led to some rather ridiculous circumstances as Prince Onyemachi describes "when it came to prize giving my name was called and I was told to do a lap as there were so many items to read out."

The time taken to announce the awards was solved from 1994 by publishing a list and then just calling the boys out to receive their badges and credits, separate presentations being made for the company awards such as Esprit d'corps, best drilled private etc.

The prize of a free camp for esprit d'corps and the attempted vote rigging by some boys was worthy of many a dubious aspiring politician but the boys themselves were normally too shrewd to let their votes be purchased. It's fair to say that in most years the officers ensured that fair play prevailed.

Between 1994 and 1999 the company and senior section strength averaged over 40 boys numerically giving the company its highest strength since the mid 1960's. These relatively high numbers were not matched by an increase in officer strength in that there were just three officers to manage not only these two groups but also a junior section averaging 15 boys. This meant a rethink in how things were done particularly as despite the numbers boys were often unwilling to come out more than one night a week. This meant that that on Fridays the company section started earlier at 6.30 with seniors not coming down until 8.00pm and in 1998 the target squad (first year company section boys) met with the junior section. The volume of badge work on a Friday grew as the following range of badge credits awarded in 1997 shows: music, drill, Christian faith, leadership, bible knowledge, computers, hobbies, gym, crime prevention, road safety, map making, fire prevention, sportsman, physical recreation and expedition. Another change on a Friday from 1996 onwards was the move toward a sweatshirt uniform, this was essential with physical activities such as gym now being on a Friday night. One added facility that the company had from 1994 which helped to cope with the extra numbers was an outdoor all weather ball court with flood lighting which enabled a group of boys to go out to let off steam whilst the other staff worked with another age group. Although the size of the area meant that on occasion it was used as an outdoor drill hall.

Bible Class was still a key feature of the company with attendance being a membership requirement .Attendance was not always what it could be as the 1996 annual reports says "Bible Class attendance has been patchy, with a hard core of boys attending, However turn out at church parades has been good." This latter point is echoed by Rev. Brian Stevens who was Chaplain in the mid 1990's and who says "As a pastor & chaplain it was always good to see the boys on church parade. What was impressive was not only the numbers but the generally good behaviour of the boys. It was not always set at their level because there was such a wide age range- to cater for, -but they managed the parades well~ Nowhere was this-more noticeable than at the Remembrance Day Service. They showed a lot of respect for those who had died in the wars. They displayed a lot of dignity."

During the late 1990's whilst the church was without a minister the number of parades was reduced as these notes from the annual reports from 1998 report "but only five church parades have been held, with a variable attendance." 1999 showed a similar picture with only four parades.

Throughout the 1990's the junior section was led by Jim Ballard numbers varied between 10 and 25 a providing a steady stream of recruits for the Company section the 1995 annual report said " The junior section this year has benefited from having a regular pro- gramme of activities and a regular turnout of boys with an average of 25 boys meeting each Wednesday . The growth in the section means that we will have 12 boys promoted to the company section, our largest number for over 10 years. The section has also had two specials outing to Megabowl and Zap zone last summer and ice hockey in February." The following years report states that "The Junior section has undertaken a wide range of activities and achieve- ments which is reflected in the awards gained by the boys. Most Wednesdays there is a regular number of between 16 and 22 boys carrying out games achievements and craft activities together with a regular devotional time."

The junior section were also regular participants in the London dis- trict junior section 11 aside football competition reaching the final three times (1993,1994,1995) each time to be beaten by the 2nd Ruislip, in the last two years by the odd goal . The third game was the most one sided 1-0 defeat on record, the 2nd had 1 shot and scored the 70th did everything else but score. The 70th did eventually get a share of the trophy in 1998 in a drawn final 1-1 the last year the event was played . After that year juniors under 10 were no longer allowed to play 11 aside football and the competition changed to seven a side.

The company and senior boys had an unprecedented level of success in London competitions throughout the decade. The most enduring memories come from two competitions. The first of these was the district senior five aside football competition and event dominated by the 70th since it was first played in 1992 when the finalists were the 70th A v 70th B . The A team won. Victories followed in the next three years that were all played indoors, in 1996 the event moved outdoors to Battersea park and the 70th almost lost the competition before the final narrowly winning a penalty shoot out. The following year saw the 70th retain the trophy for the fifth

year beating the 5th Croydon 3-0 with a team that included two boys who both went onto play in the Premiership -Gavin Holligan and Nathan Ellington, the latter playing in goal as he was injured, one wonders what the score might have been if they were both on the pitch. For the record the trophy was also won in 1998 and 1999. The other activity was Athletics where the 70th provided most or if not all the Battalion team that won the London Competition between 1995 and 1999, the outstanding memory of all the running, jumping and throwing from those years is that of Giles Palmer storming through to victory, or so he thought, in a sprint finish of the 1500 metres that saw him come from 4th to 1st only to hear the bell sound, he had miscounted and had one lap left to go , having given his all he then had to chase after the pack again eventually finishing third.

The company's involvement in the national competitions gave the senior boys a sense of achievement and team work which made up for the absence of local events and the lack of a relevant badge structure for the 15 plus age group if they didn't want to work for their Queens badge. It also assisted in retaining and even recruiting members, so the company somewhat unusually at the time always had a double figure number of seniors and a regular number of members being discharged at the age limit. However despite what may be thought of as a predominance of sport, life in the 70th in the 1990's was more than that as Stephen Rock notes. "What cemented things was not just football and sport. It was a collection of friends. We all acted like a family and a community here. We all got on really well with each other not just on a Friday but during the week and

the weekend. MY social circle was the BB and I introduced others to it. There was also the big selling point to my mum of the church base."

During the 1990's national finals were reached with regularity .The volleyball and five a side football finals were reached in 1990, 1991 and 1992 each time the Company returned empty handed always being the best placed English team but failing to beat the Scots and the Irish even when the finals was played in England. There was per-haps a sense of frustration in the Captain's report to the 1991 display which concluded when referring to the two finals . "In both cases we were beaten not due to lack of skill but mainly to inadequate team-work and training. It is my firm belief that the Company will only win a national trophy when its members are prepared to knuckle down to a higher level of preparation and discipline than that which is currently accepted by the boys."

The 1992 football finals was of particular note not for the result but for the experience of the first "overseas excursion" with a visit to Northern Ireland . The team flew over to Belfast and then experi-enced an unusual minibus trip to Londonderry where the finals were being played. The bus was a converted transit van with bench seats and no windows . The driver apologized for the traffic jams of three cars in front of him at the lights and it was a surreal experience being in part of the United Kingdom with armed soldiers on streets and some amazing murals. After the finals in which we were duly beaten in the semi finals we stayed with the 1st Knocknamuckley company and stayed in the church hall at Portadown. Unfortunately the hosts hadn't advised the local police we were staying there and the light on after midnight and some noise attracted the local police but the shadows of three armed men walking around the building and then appearing at the rear door led to the boys hiding under the stage with their eyes out like organ stops. Fortunately, the RUC believed who we were and also they were who they said they were not someone else. After a superb full Ulster breakfast we then visited Portadown itself and it was amazing to see that the local boys took the periodic bombing of the main street as if it was an everyday event. We finished the Sunday evening in church and then the boys joint some of the locals hanging around in the car park -something they did as a regular routine . The following day on the Monday stomachs stabilised by yet another full Ulster fry up it was back in the windowless van to Belfast and the fly home, a weekend never to be forgotten.

In 1993 we again reached both finals the Volleyball in Glasgow was memorable for the trip up and back. Normally we would travel to Scotland by train, for some reason we couldn't get tickets at the required time so we reverted to coach which meant an overnight trip up, then the coach tickets became like gold dust as the railway men declared a one day strike on the date we were due to travel. If we hadn't pre-booked the coach we would have missed Scotland. Some might call it coincidence but perhaps it was someone looking over us. Perhaps this time we could blame the journey but the result in the volleyball was the same.

Visit to Londonderry 1992

The five a side football finals were in Nottingham and an early morning meet up and a minibus drive to the University saw us arrive a lot fresher than we had been in Glasgow less than a month previously. However our first game saw everything go wrong and we lost 3-1, the first half of the next game was similar bit something then clicked and that was won 6-1, the third game was also won and we were back in the semi finals. That was won 2-1 a tight affair and we were in the final against the 2nd Cambusnethan again a tight game but after a nervy first half we scored two second half goals to win 2-0, national champions at last. As a treat the whole squad and spectators went to an up market Pizza restaurant to celebrate, the looks on the other customers were somewhat wary when they saw a dozen boisterous black boys enter the restaurant. Looks that were not completely unjustified when Jabbu Siphika got struck by cramp halfway through a Pizza eating competition almost knocking the whole table over and bringing the restaurant to a stunned silence. Virtually the same squad then won a borough wide tournament for all youth groups in July of that year proving that Nottingham was no fluke.

1997 saw the 70th winning a second national final, travelling down the M4 to Swindon the team played some stylish but robust football to reach the semi final where as the report in the company newsletter records it "In the semi final the 10th Inverness provided a physical opposition but were beaten 3-0, as were last years winners the 4th Portadown in the final 4-1". The comment about the final doesn't mention that the game was effectively over within the 1st minute with the 70th being 2-0 up and the playing keep ball for much of the game.

In addition the success in football and volleyball the company also had success in a new competition which replaced volleyball, this was badminton an event previously just practiced for leisure but now played in competition. The company reached the finals in 1998 where we also hosted the event. However, our experience like in Volleyball was that although we could beat the English teams to qualify our efforts floundered against the Scots and Irish. Throughout the 1990's the company also took part in the Table Tennis, chess and Masterquiz events surprising themselves in 1996 when they reached the semi final of the latter. Much of the travel around England to get to these events was by minibus usually driven by Barry Green and as Marlon Bailey says " Barry must have driven us two or three times round the country in that green minibus."

 One summer activity that the boys both enjoyed and endured was expedition work for the bronze and silver level of the Duke of Edinburgh's award. Unfortunately no one reached gold. An enduring moment for some of the boys in 1993 as they were doing their expedition in Surrey was as they crossed a road looking to one side and seeing the company minibus having been put through 180 degrees onto its roof with the captain sitting unscathed beside it. Their concerns were not for the health of the driver more for "how are we going to get home tomorrow!"

In the early 1990's the London District display was held at the Wembley Conference Centre, with the 37th having closed the 70th took over the job of being arena orderlies in the three displays that were held there in 1990,1991 and 1993. This would have been straight forward on the first one except that it clashed with the national five a side football finals and the birth of the captain's third child. So a much depleted 70th with some help from the ex 37th staff managed to carry out the days duties to a good enough standard such that they were invited back the following year.

The last London district display was in 1993 and the 70th were there in three categories as arena orderlies, taking part in a junior section games item with other companies in the battalion involving various cones, wheelbarrows, bricks and planks in an item called "South Circular" and lastly with the steel band giving it's inaugural performance, but more about that later. Nathan Asare Comments that " We did so many things that we would never have done outside. Arena orderlies at Wembley conference centre. We all enjoyed it, just being there. It was not just the sport but all the wider stuff we did."

During the 1990's the company took part in a number of one off special events. For instance in 1990 at the invitation of Ann Heyward, who played piano at Bible Class for a number of years, the company were asked to put on a gym item for a Save the Children's fund function in Roehampton where the special guest was HRH the Princess Royal, Princess Anne. The boys of varying gymnastic ability were stride vaulting over the box as the Princess came in. Unfortunately the one photograph taken for the press shows Wayne Henry doing a good Concorde impersonation. Wayne was a brilliant basketball player but at boxwork it was A for effort only.

In 1994 the Brigade held a special review to mark the retirement of

TOOTING Boy's Brigade gymnastics team displayed their supple movements for Princess Anne. Wayne Henry, 16, is picuted vaulting over the horse.

the outgoing Brigade President Viscount Thurso. (Lord Thurso had previously paid a visit to the company in 1988 to watch a round of top of the form .) Eight 70th members were invited to take part in the Royal review which took place at Windsor Castle in front of Her Majesty the Queen. This event was filmed and 70th members can be briefly seen in it being inspected by her Majesty. Two of the boys who took part both in the gym item as well as the Royal review were Stephen Rock and Nathan Asare both of whom clearly remember both events. Nathan says " It was great, it is something that we would never have done before or since, meeting the Queen." Stephen adds "My drill was never that perfect but it meant a lot to me, marching out at Windsor to meet the Queen."

The company was asked in October 1986 to take part in the annual Founder's day ceremony at St Paul's Cathedral where there is a memorial in the crypt to the Founder Sir William Smith . After sitting through evensong, which to say the least was a bit different to bible class members laid a wreath at the Founder's memorial.

Another trip to central London took place a few months later when in a fund raiser for company funds a dozen boys saw how quickly they could visit the monopoly board in real life starting at the Old Kent Rd and finishing in Mayfair, although not visiting every site in order the boys raised over £400 whilst improving their knowledge of how to get round London by bus, tube and foot. They finished the day tired but happy knowing that getting to Mayfair was worth the £400!.

With the closure of the bugle band in 1989 the 70th were without any musical activity. In 1992, following an approach from the then London District Secretary Richard Davis, the company were approached as to whether we would like a set of steel pans that used to belong to the 104th London who had closed in 1991. Simultaneously the Girls Brigade captain had also expressed a view that a steel band would be a good joint activity for both groups and thus pans and idea were brought together. Instruction was initially provided by Ken George a member at St James Church and the first performance was at the church carol service in December 1992. During 1993 and 1994 the band gradually built up its repertoire and performed mainly at local school fetes, church events and similar local functions. From the beginning transport was provided by John Elliott who was a willing volunteer for head driver and roadie assisted by Barry Green and the company captain. Being the driver could present its own difficulties : in one incident John became separate from the band and driving a battered white transit van drove into the ring of steel around the City of London, with only large metal containers visible, he somehow managed to persuade the armed police that despite his Irish accent he was delivering a steel band to the Drapers Hall and not a few hundred pounds of mixed fertilizer or semtex!

By 1996 the band was playing up to twenty events a year and in that year alone performed before HRH Prince of Wales when he visited Phipps Bridge estate in Mitcham. At the Royal Albert Hall in May the band played as part of an item presented by the 7th London at the Girls Brigade National rally. The tunes played on that occasion included "lambada and Hot, hot, hot" whilst the girls were dressed in bright colourful carnival costumes with an elaborate dance routine. The band were back at the GB rally the following year providing the backing music for the London District Gym team. The summer schedule was hectic as this extract from May 1997 company newsletter shows

"Did you see and hear the band on the BBC's coverage of the London Marathon, if you missed them then catch them at one of the following events:
May 10th : GB rally, Royal Albert Hall; May 24th Queen Mary's hospital, Carshalton ; May 31st: International Jazz day, Morden park; June 7th : Southfields Festival; June 8th Leukaemia Research - Battersea Park ; June 14th Mid Surrey Fun day -Nonsuch Park (am); Roehampton Festival (pm) ; June 21st -Alton Towers ; June 28th - Chelsea Royal Hospital - beating retreat."

Playing near the Cutty Sark on the route of the London Marathon was a regular occurrence from 1997 and an early morning start was essential to ensure that the band was in place before the roads closed and the race started. Once the runners started it was not untypical for the band to have to play for 90 minutes non stop both to keep the crowd and the runners going but it did play havoc with the wrists. 1998 saw the band make two appearances out of the usual both of which were at the back of August, a time when the band was nor- mally resting. These two appearances were at the Notting Hill carni- val and then the weekend after at Brigade Council. The appearance at Notting Hill was as part of a worship service on the Sunday Morning whilst the Brigade Council appearance was as part of The London show event at the Orchard theatre, Dartford. This again involved a dance item involving some of the junior section boys and junior girls using some of the costumes from the Royal Albert Hall two years earlier. Many of those who took part as dancers became learner members of the band the following session.

As the following extract from the 1998 annual report shows the band was extremely popular. "The joint BB and GB steel band "Kool Drummings" has continued with a busy programme of local and national performances including church services with over 20 appearances since last years display and more booked well into 1999.In fact we have so many requests to play that we have to turn down almost 50% of the requests due to previous engagements. We purchased additional pans, this has enabled us to give more members the opportunity to learn and play outside." The following year was less busy but the band grew in popularity with its membership now up to 20 as the 1999 annual report shows. "The band has made 15 appearances in the past 12 months from places as far apart as Brighton and Cromer. The band membership is currently 20 and operates with the assistance of a tutor provided by the London Borough of Wandsworth. The band provides the opportunity for the boys and girls to express themselves musically and to get in a fair degree of travelling. The band has recently been enhanced with a percussion section. The band was self funding over the years with money from fees covering running costs such as vehicle hire and insurance whilst grants provided for equipment replacement.

At the end of July or the beginning of August each year the company continued to camp. With the demise of the 37th, the 70th camps gradually became a single company camp although a few boys from the 2nd Herne Bay continued to camp with the company until 1994 and we did have one or two boys from the 28th and 99th London as well. The company was only able to camp because of assistance from old boys, parents and others who supplemented the company officers to provide sufficient staff to run a camp for seven days. Two regular faces were Brian Prichard as camp medical officer and John Elliott as camp cook, also throughout his ministry at Tooting Rev. Brian Stevens was at camp .His comment about camp is as follows "Then there were the camps. The boys did basically get along well together. They enjoyed the competitions, not only football but believe it or not also the tent inspection. The camps gave good opportunities to have more personal talks with them and certainly they knew all about the gospel at the end of the week. Another memorable thing was the staff suppers. Not only was the site fairly quiet but the staff could relax and eat and eat. During my time as chaplain we were fortunate enough to be in the age of the deep fried Mars bars. No boy was allowed to indulge, this was for staff only!"

Camp in 1990 saw the 70th return to Swanage, Dorset, for the first time since 1966 . The field was in the grounds of the old grammar school to the North of the town and had the benefits of no cow pats or long grass but still had the delights of chemical toilets and cold water washing but it did have access to electricity supply rigged up from the main school building. 1991 saw a move to Tenby in South Wales using a traditional field our own canvas and grass about four inches high . The site had access by a very short walk to a long sandy beach where for some reason the boys wanted to play American football which was fashionable that year. One of the days out involved a trip to a local leisure park where amongst the attractions were Go Karts which were popular with the boys and with staff until the latter were banned for reckless driving. We also, for some reason visited the local power station .

1992 saw a return to the 1990 site at Swanage .Camp fell at the same time as the Olympics and the camp gathered around the TV as the sports programme was suspended to watch Linford Christie in the 100 metres final . However at the same time the TV was plugged in there was a power cut which took out half of Swanage leaving the boys to listen to the radio whilst staring at a blank screen in the vain hope that the power would come back on. That year's camp cross country was to say the least chaotic with somehow the runners being split into three groups en route with the two oldest runners Owen Clark as Chaplain and Brian Prichard as MO claiming victory as they arrived back at the site first.

The following year saw a return to Whitecliff Bay on the Isle of Wight. The same site as used in the late 1980's. For the first time in a number of years the boys, according to their tents, were sent on a night hike being dropped off at various points in the area and given a time limit to be back by midnight. Come midnight the first two tents were literally marched back into the camp field by Micah Archer.The other tents followed in until only one was left . At 1.30am a worried C.O. and Padre went out in the minibus looking for them and found them minus their tent commander outside of Brading .When asked where the tent commander was they pointed back up the road where a rather sodden Jabbu Siphika stood. Evidently, he was so convinced that he was leading his tent the right way that he had led from the front and stepped straight into the River Yar, which fortunately was only knee high. The stench was such that he had to be literally hosed down with cold water round the back of the marquee before his boys would let him back into the tent. Other adventure activities that year included water sports and mountain biking. The minigolf tournament was also noted for a crack on the head to one boy from a golf club that somehow the Prof managed to stop the bleeding without stitches.

1994 saw a return to Devon, this time to Teignmouth using the playing fields of the local secondary school .This gave access to proper flush loos . The site had it's own football pitch which on one occasion was invaded by the local team who had come in for some pre season training .This led to a bit of an argument which unfortunately corresponded with a visit from the inspecting officer who mistook the shouting for camp indiscipline!

Later that evening whilst the boys were playing the staff at football the game was finished in a mist with the boys claiming that they couldn't see as the C.O. knee'd the ball past the keeper.

1995 Camp was again in Devon above the town of Dartmouth, this time at the grounds of the Community college high above the town, the camp started with one of the minibuses breaking down just outside of Stonehenge and having to be towed all the way to Dartmouth with boys and luggage. The vehicle wasn't fixed for most of the week but we were still able to enjoy a full programme which included a trip to Devenport dockyards. The site also had the luxury of showers. Despite the modern comforts the boys still had the age old routine of reveille at 6.30am, tent inspection including rolling the brailing and belt cleaning before breakfast and then morning prayers.

Camp returned to the Isle of Wight in 1996, no showers or posh loos, just cold water and chemicals and another broken down minibus involving the vehicle this time being towed from outside Guildford to Southampton on to the ferry and into the camp site. However, there was a degree of indiscipline amongst the senior boys following one officially approved late night out where the boys overstayed their welcome in a local establishment .After a summary fair trial the subsequent choice of punishment for the four boys concerned was either a trip home, or a confinement to camp for three days combined with three one hour lectures from the Prof on the evils of alcohol. The latter was chosen.

1997 camp returned to Swanage area using a third site, that at the Middle School, again complete with mod cons. The annual report for the year has the following comment "Camp last year was a great event despite the weather, a full range of activities was provided including canoeing, karting, rope work and climbing. Our camp chaplain was Sashi Seghal who held the boys' interest during the week and ten boys made a commitment, these have been followed up." The year was also notable apart from four days of continuous rain to the moving of the main devotional to after the evening meal not after supper. From the boys response something must have worked but the experiment wasn't continued.

Dartmouth was revisited in 1998 and the main memory of that week was when a strong wind blew up on the day most of the camp was 30 miles away at Devonport .The three staff left struggled manfully to peg the tents down .However, the beauty of mobile technology meant that most of the rest of the staff got back quickly to assist whilst the boys were oblivious to this, enjoying an extended dip in the local swimming pool. The year's annual report records. "Camp last year … a full range of activities was provided including, karting, a visit to Devonport Docks and water sports. The chaplain's duties were shared by the staff."

1999 saw a return to Sussex for the first time since the 1970's this time camping at Ringmer near Lewes. The annual report for the year reported briefly on that camp as follows "One traditional activity that has just been completed is our annual camp, this year 23 boys travelled to Ringmer in East Sussex using our own canvas, activities undertaken included Go-karting, golf, mountain biking, laser quest, bowling and swimming."

During the decade the number and level of out of camp activities increased. This was made possible partly due to external funding but also to the mobility provided by minibuses. The main effect it had on the traditional camp programme was that the main meal moved to the evening slot. A typical 1990's camp day was as follows:

Reveille 6.30am ; orderly squad start 7.00am ; tent inspection 7.50am ; breakfast followed by morning prayers 8.10am ; morning activity 9.30 am ; packed lunch or sandwiches 1.00pm ; afternoon activity ; evening meal 5.00pm; camp sports 6.30pm ; supper followed by evening prayers 9.00pm ; lights out 10.15pm.

What had also changed was the camp menu . Breakfast was porridge or a choice of cereals followed by a some fried variant normally with beans ; evening meals became more exotic with a range of English and continental meals including spaghetti bolognese, roast chicken, rice and peas and chicken, lamb curry, chicken stir fry with spare ribs and rice and toad in the hole with mash. No camp menu was complete without duff for pudding which was normally followed by the camp cross country. The packed lunches were also filled out with cakes provided by either parents or church members. It has to be said that some of the cakes because of the additional preservatives had to be held back from the boys and the camp drivers.

It is difficult to try and compare the monetary value of a camp between generations however the table below gives some comparison between camp 1948 and camp 1998. Perhaps the biggest surprise is the cost of activities provided to the boys of 1998.

	1948 cost per head	1948 at 1998 prices Cost per head	1998 cost per head
food	£1.06	£21.83	£17.18
site & equipment hire	£0.64	£13.23	£20.77
equipment purchase	£0.11	£2.27	£5.46
transport	£0.52	£10.75	£22.88
fuel	£0.02	£0.41	£2.77
sundry	£0.16	£3.31	£2.27
activities	0	£0	£24.39
COST PER HEAD	£2.51	£51.80	£95.72
CHARGE per head	£1.95	£40.31	£77.50

1998 saw the company's 90th anniversary and as with other years a reunion was held on the day of the display however as the annual report describes "This years old boys reunion was a happy event but attendance was lower than expected both from newer and older old boys". It is also fair to say that the same applied to the display and the following year the company took the unusual step of not holding a display.

In fact 1999 was a year with a number of changes as set out in the annual report for that year recorded below:- "The company has undertaken a full range of activities over the past year. Meeting on three nights of the week and at weekends. The company continues to operate three age groups juniors (age 8-11), company age (11-14) and seniors (15-18) . At the end of August membership of the three sections was 14, 12 and 18 respectively. This is a slight decrease over the same period last year. This change in membership has bought its own challenges and from September we have been tri-alling for the 14+ age group a new programme called senior plus . This will involve a mix of on and offsite activities.

During the past year we have however continued with a mix of badge work, physical activity, social activities and a spiritual pro-gramme with Bible class at 11.00am which now includes members of the Girls' Brigade and devotions on Wednesdays and Fridays. Activities have included gymnastics, photography, crime prevention, cooking, visit to Alton Towers, a study on the application of the ten commandments today, Road safety & expedition work, among many other activities. The Company has worked closely with the Girls' Brigade company on a number of events and activities for instance providing for a Local Authority awards ceremony and the joint steel band Kool Drummings.

The company continues to give members the opportunity to achieve on both an individual and corporate basis. Three boys have achieved their Presidents badge while four boys have achieved Bronze Duke of Edinburgh's award status. On a wider front the company has won the following London District events -Five a side football, 11 a side football, athletics, Gymnastics, Pr games, six aside cricket and 11 a

side cricket. On a national basis they came within a whisker of qualifying for the United Kingdom badminton and five a side football
Finals. The Junior Section also won the local area Football and
swimming competitions. These and the other competitions in which
we were unsuccessful give our members a varied range of physical
activities in which they can compete.

The company continues to draw on an ethnically mixed population
with the boys parents coming from a over 15 different nationalities.
This wide variety of backgrounds presents its own challenges which
help to make the 70th a place where boys want to come, mix and
develop.

The Company has also tried to play its part in the wider community
and has been involved in a number of charity events with the steel
band and has taken part in the Brigade's national appeal to purchase
four lifeboats raising £200. Financially, the company has been self
sufficient and this year no direct appeal has been made to church
members for support. However, fund raising externally does present
a constant challenge both in terms of time and ideas.

As we enter a new millenium the company staff are consistently
looking at ways in which our work with the boys can be updated to
reflect the interests of today's boys and young men without losing
the ethos of The Boys' Brigade in terms of discipline and spiritual
development. We intend to build on the achievements of the past
while looking to the future."

The changes referred to in the report were largely brought about by
external circumstances . For instance the change in Bible class was a
result in no Sunday school teachers being available within the
church whilst the other changes were due to staff shortages.
However, these changes did have a marked affect on the way that the
Company could operate in the following decade.

The new Millenium.2000-2008

The Company entered the 21st century looking at new challenges whilst still trying to remain true to its roots. The Brigade as a whole was going through yet more change perhaps the most significant of which was to phase out the haversack and belt which had born worn since the first BB uniform was designed and replace them with two alternative uniforms a polo / sweatshirt variant and a shirt and tie variant, in addition the officers said good bye to the Glengarry hat, blue suit and brown lapel badges. The attached extract for the year 2000 annual report gives some idea of life in the company

"The past twelve months has been a year of transition for the company, with changes to days and programmes in two of the three sections. It is perhaps too early to see if the effects of these changes will be beneficial in the long run, but the changes have been to some extent forced due to the age structure of the membership and the limited staffing resources available to the company. At the current time membership stands at 40. With 13 juniors, 10 company & 17 seniors. This is after six seniors reached the age limit at the end of the session. The former group meeting on Wednesdays with the latter two on Fridays. The company & junior sections have throughout the year carried out a more traditional programme of badge work and other activities with the results reflected in the list of badges & credits being awarded at the display tonight. The wide range of activities reflects the whole spectrum of brigade work.

The company has not neglected the spiritual side of things with regular devotions in the week and Bible Class on Sunday mornings, the latter is shared with the GB. Attendance at this meeting is patchy and consideration needs to be given to whether this arrangement is suitable for the whole of the 11-18 year age group. Another joint activity with more girls than boys this time is the steel band. This is in great demand and has made just under 20 appearances in the past 12 months and is fully booked over the summer. The band is taught by Paul Dowie, who has introduced a number of new tunes and arrangements over the past year. However Paul left us at the end of the year.

On the competition front the company has had a mixed year winning the London district five-a-side football, six & eleven a side football and basketball. In addition we have been runners up in the district cross country, junior section football & gym. In the five national competitions the company had a degree of success in the badminton reaching the English final where we lost on a playoff, and in the UK five a side finals where we were beaten in the group stages 1-0 by the eventual winners the 3rd Airdrie.

Camp this year was at Swanage in Dorset and a wide range of activities including go karting, ropes & mountain biking took place.

This year's display in May was a more relaxed occasion which was unfortunately matched with a relaxed turnout. However the boys were able to show off some of their activities. The turnout from church members was disappointing.

The company has provided stewards for a civic occasion with the GB while the band has played at a number of charitable events.

The work of the Company is entirely dependent upon the voluntary activity of the officers and staff both in terms of day to day programme and annual camp and without this voluntary donation of time both during the evenings and at weekends the level of activity achieved would not be possible. We look forward to the new year with anticipation and hope to continue our new programme for Seniors and develop new programmes for our younger members."

Amongst the band performances was a high profile performance at the millennium dome in front of some 20000+ visitors on an October half term, the acoustics it has to be said were really something even if the exhibits left something to be desired. At the end of August the band also played as part of the Brigade Council held at Brighton on this occasion the band played as dusk fell on the seafront and then carried on playing in the pitch dark as the lights went out and stayed out for some 15 minutes.

The company strength of 40 overall needs to be taken in the context of an average London company   in 2000 being 28 boys broken down as follows 8 anchors, 10 juniors, 7 company and 3 seniors. As far as the battalion was concerned this was now down to six companies with even the 88th London closing with some of their numbers moving to the 70th.

The poor turn out of an audience at the display led to the Company trying an open evening approach in 2001 but this again failed to attract a lot of interest and because of this no further displays were held. Numbers stayed fairly static in 2001 but the company did have a high degree of competition success as the 2001 annual report repeated below shows. The year also marked another first when we camped under canvas with the GB for the first time. This experiment worked well and was repeated in 2002 and 2003. Although a joint camp the two companies only really came together for some activities and evening devotions. Tent inspection, morning devotions and meals were kept separate using two different marquees and it was really more like two camps on one site rather than a joint camp.

"In the past twelve months the Company has had a significant year of achievement both in terms of competitions and also in terms of work undertaken .This is despite the limited staffing resources available to the company. At the end of the session (August) membership stood at 13 juniors, 10 company & 18 seniors. The former group meeting on Wednesdays with the latter two on Fridays. The company & junior sections have throughout the year carried out a programme of badge work and other activities with the results reflected in a wide range of credits & badges gained. The wide range of activities reflects the whole spectrum of brigade work and has included art work, craft, expedition work, as well as a wide range of physical activity.

The company has not neglected the spiritual side of things with regular devotions in the week and Bible Class on Sunday mornings, the latter is shared with the GB. Another joint activity with more girls than boys this time is the steel band. This is in great demand and has made a wide range of appearances at both local & regional level. Achieving good press coverage for the company.

On the competition front the company has had its most successful year ever: Winning nine London district titles, A district record these were: the Senior five a side football, senior eleven a side football, junior six a side football, cross country, athletics, team & individual groundwork, six a side cricket & basketball. In addition we have been runners up in the under 14 five aside football, & the Pr games and third in the vaulting. In the five National Competitions we for the third year in succession were beaten at the final English stage in the badminton However, in the UK five a side finals where we were unbeaten in all five matches played and won the final, beating the 11th Coatbridge 5-0. This was our third victory in less than 10 years. A competition record.

Camp this year was at Ringmer in Sussex and was held in conjunction with our Girls Brigade Company, over 30 young people took part in a wide range of activities including go karting, ropes, canoeing, bowling, rock climbing, golf & mountain Biking took place. This activity could not take part without the fifteen volunteers who staffed the camp. Our chaplain Rev. Alistair Clark led the devotions following, which a number of enquires were made about the Christian faith.

Instead of a display this year we held an open evening. This year was a relaxed occasion which gave the boys the opportunity boys were able to show off some of there activities and to gain credit for the hard work put in throughout the session.

Turning to the current session we hope to continue our programme for Seniors who will be looking at developing a Company Web site in the next twelve months and to continue to develop new programmes for our younger members who are showing a good deal of potential which we hope to develop in the next twelve months. However, since August we have had a slight down turn in numbers with a drop in Juniors & seniors but a slight increase in Company boys. We intend to rectify this by a recruiting campaign in the Spring . One change in the programme is the Seniors Bible Class on a Sunday afternoon -"The Difference". This programme is using Youth Alpha material at present and has had a mixed response from the senior boys .

It was good to see a number of former members at the reunion in October and we would hope to hold another reunion in the future. The support of former members either financially or in prayer is much appreciated.

In many respects 2002 has the opportunity to be a defining year for the company. There are boys out in the community who are no doubt interested and whose parents would welcome the influence of the BB . However, it is not just our job as BB staff to recruit & retain them it is the job of the whole church, as we are only appointed by you to undertake this task on your behalf . We must make sure that the environment to which we invite them is not only welcoming to them but also to there families and that we do not hinder them by what we do or say from coming to us or put barriers in their way to coming to us"

Two band highlights not mentioned in the report were in October when Kool drummings played as part of the district centenary event at St Paul's Cathedral and at the end of year the band played at the same function as a chart topper, not the Spice Girls or Robbie Williams but Bob the Builder.

The last paragraph of the report hints at the degree of frustration felt by the staff at the time about as they saw it the church's, inability to want to deal with the challenges that a new generation of youngsters and their families presented.

Despite the comment made in the 2001 annual report 2002 was probably more a year for marking time rather than more definition. One significant event was the reducing numbers of juniors . This meant that it was no longer viable to continue to operate a section with less than half a dozen boys and the decision was made to move them to a Thursday where the boys could operate partially by them-selves and partly with the Girls Brigade. Over time this arrangement worked and the number of junior boys gradually rose. However, despite this increase in numbers this joint working with separate identities was continued.

Camp in 2002 saw the company again using the same site as the Girls Brigade this time on the Isle of Wight as we returned to Whitecliff Bay. The arrangements were similar to those in 2001 with some activities mixed but inspection and morning prayers being undertaken separately. This site was the first time since 1996 that we had not used a school playing field .Unfortunately the farmer had not mown the grass and thus it was virtually impossible to play games or walk safely in some areas .So two mowers were hired and the tent areas, football pitch and other areas were cut to size with the grass being bundled up by boys on extra orderlies. The camp also had a visit from the mayor of Wandsworth who drove into the field in the mayoral limo.

In competitions the company was less successful losing its national five a side football title in a play off in the last qualifying round but winning in a new title in the first ever England and Wales under 14 outdoor five a side football finals . The company also won the London athletics entering for the first time as a company team, the senior five a side football, vaulting and the six-a-side cricket. This was the last time this trophy was played for as it followed the 11 aside cricket and senior 11 a side football into the history books. Both of the cricket competitions suffered in part because of the new safety requirements for teenage cricket involving the wearing of helmets.

Despite the disappointment in the five-a-side football the company did reach another national final that of the Badminton where the teamed travelled to Manchester and also reached the semi final of the Masterteam quiz competition .

For this session eleven a side football meant playing in the Bromley battalion league and cup and travelling down to Orpington most Saturdays and winning both competitions. This involved a reasonably high standard of football but a minimum of at least one hour each way travel just to get to and from the game.

Kool drummings continued to play throughout 2002 and as in previous years the number of requests for performances exceeded the number of engagements. During the year the senior members of the band became the band tutors and music arrangers. Being the Queen's Golden Jubilee year there were a number of performances with a jubilee theme. However one event the band missed, they had a prior booking, was taking part in the BB float in the parade down the Mall, the vehicle for the float was acquired by the Company captain and driven by the every dependable John Elliott within a few feet of the Queen in the Mall with BB boys from the district on the back .

A typical weekly programme for 2002 was a follows
>Bible Class Sundays 11.00am
>Steel band practice Monday 7.00pm
>Badminton practise Wednesday 6.45pm
>Junior section -Thursdays 6.00pm
>Company & senior sections Friday 6.30pm
>Football - Saturdays

The activities of the company also received a degree of outside interest both from inside and outside the Brigade as these extracts from the October 2002 company newsletter show,
"We have been involved in a few activities outside the normal range of things. In September we were involved in two weeks of video production for The BB at national level . Evidently some of our activities are regarded as being outside the normal scope of things and thus we were selected to take part in the video which will be distributed to all BB companies in the UK showing what sorts of activities BB companies can do

A couple of weeks later some of the seniors together with the GB seniors and Brigaders were interviewed by researchers for their views on crime and relationships with the police. Four members (two girls /two boys) then made a presentation to the partnership board which was well received.

Apart from the above we also took part in a special five a side football tournament organised by the Reading Stedfast association winning both the under 16 and over 16 age groups."

The Company also continued with a wide range of badge work and enabled boys to work towards the highest awards the BB could offer the Presidents and queens badge, helping others   and take part in leading parade services as well as taking part in competitive events as the following extracts from Company newsletters note .

"In December the company assisted the Girls Brigade in leading the Parade service . This was a truly memorable and first rate effort and we look forward to there next Service. The Concert for autism awareness was attended by over 100 people and £300 was raised for this cause. Well done to all who took part. An oversight from the December Newsletter was the fact that seven boys attended and completed there leadership 3 course, which will lead in time to seven Presidents badges and possibly some Queens Men."

Unfortunately, in common with many of the company members who worked for the Queens badge in the badge structure after 1968 the Queens badge was perhaps a step too far .

The following year continued in much the same vein of busyness as this extract from the Spring newsletter shows.

"In the national competitions we had mixed news; In the semi final of the under 14 five aside football we won all five games and qualified for the finals on May 31st - more details next month .. In the table tennis we were beaten in the 4th round 8-1 by 4th Barking . The badminton team were beaten in a play off by the 1st Barnet after a 3-3 tie . They now qualify for the final.In the London competitions it was a case of so near but so far. In The PR games we came second as we did in the vaulting and mat work competitions. In the Senior five a side team despite remaining unbeaten we lost out on goal difference to register our 4th second of the month. Overall the efforts of the boys were not reflected in the positions.
In addition to the competition programme we still found time for the steel band to play at the Wandsworth Young person of the year award."

The apparent lack of success at London level was followed up in the National arena, in May the under 14 five aside team made two trips to Nottingham, in the first they narrowly failed to retain their England and Wales trophy being beaten 1-0 in the final .However at the end of the month they were back again this time playing indoors and winning the inaugural United Kingdom under 14 five a side football competition. This event was played in a league format and the team came back from losing it's first game 2-1 so that it knew that a 2-0 win in the last game would clinch the title on goal difference . A 4-0 win secured the 4th national title. The company's overall competition record meant that it was in a good position to win the revamped "Daily Telegraph Shield." This famous London district trophy had previously been held by the winners of the London three section drill competition but had not been competed for since 1992. The district decided that the trophy should instead be presented to the company with the best overall record in London and national events . In addition the number of second places recorded above wins in the basketball, athletics and cross country were enough to secure the revamped trophy which was presented at the London District Beating of Retreat at Chelsea Royal Hospital. To put the achievement in context the 70th had to beat 120 other companies to be first.

Due to staff difficulties the company was now reduced to operating on three nights with band on Mondays, juniors on Thursdays and company and senior sections on Fridays. This programme it has to be said was fairly typical within the district. Regular league football was played in 2002/3 season again travelling to Bromley . The 2003/4 season saw this reduced to just cup games. Bible Class and parades were again held although the latter varied in frequency and the former in attendance whilst the Juniors numbers were low and continued to meet with the GB. Despite the success in competitions there were underlying problems in both staffing availability and imbalance between age groups that would lead to future difficulties.

The steel band also continued to play a high number of events including yet again the London marathon, and one of their more interesting engagements a twenty first birthday party sailing down the River Thames . The Band also came to camp and played at a couple of local events . Camp itself was as in 2002 a joint affair and this year it was truly joint with virtually all activities being shared. Over 40 young people enjoyed the range of activities including karting, ropes, bikes and water sports.

September 2003 saw the company change battalion as the old South West London Battalion became defunct and so the 70th moved to the Kingston, Merton and Mid Surrey battalion whose borders were large and stretched from Chelsea and Fulham in the North to Horley near Gatwick Airport in the South. However, the size of the battalion was not reflected in the volume of activities and competitive events were again restricted mainly to London and national events and finished the year by travelling to Enfield to win both the basketball and Pr games competitions.

The company did however attempt to help others and one event where they assisted the Girls' Brigade was in a sponsored 24 hour famine where between them the young people raised some £1300. For this and winning the Daily Telegraph shield both groups were awarded the title and trophy of Wandsworth Youth group of the year.

The annual report to the church in 2004 which was joint with the Girl's Brigade took account of the fact that as many of the members were unfamiliar with the brigades that rather than detailing what happened over the year, took the time to explain to the church membership what the Brigade's functions were within the church. Some detail from that is worth repeating as it highlights the role of the BB within the church at the time.

"What do the GB & BB companies do?

The companies exist to reach young people aged between 5 and 18 and by a mixture of activities - social, interest, physical, adventure & spiritual they attempt to teach the young people about Jesus Christ and his claims on there lives.

When do they do It ?

The main evenings the companies meet are on Thursdays and Fridays, the joint band meet on Mondays and activities often take place on Saturdays. The older members come to Bible Class on a Sunday.

How many young people are involved ?

This is difficult to quantify but in any week over 60 different young people come down to one or more of these meetings. Over a year we have probably seen over 100 young people.

Where does the church fit in ?

The church is responsible for the staffing of both groups and the spiritual welfare of the staff and members . The church also provides premises.

When do we see the members ?

Members of both companies are encouraged to come down to the monthly parade services and older members to the Sunday special on the third Sunday of the month.

Are the Brigades old fashioned ?

Definitely not, the programmes both companies use are up to date and every effort is made to keep ahead of the field. The days of drill & more drill are past and modern techniques & technologies are used with the young people."

Competitions in 2004 were again mixed as the Spring newsletter shows

"In the national competitions we have reached the semi final of the under 14 five aside football winning all four games in our group. The semi final will be on April 3rd .In the London competitions it was a case of when we got our strongest team out we won, but when we failed we didn't. Our success was in the under 14 five a side foot-ball where we won all five games in the final round scoring 18 con-ceding nil. In the London cross country we came 3rd in the open event and third in the under 14 . Whilst in the box work we were second. In the eleven a side football we beat the 14th Bromley 6-0 to retain the knock out trophy. The match was closer than the score suggests"

The game against 14th Bromley was the last 11 aside game played by the company at the time of writing as from the following session 11 aside brigade football was no longer permitted by the Brigade's insurers within the whole eleven to eighteen age range and any such contact sports were thus split between 11-14 and 15-18, this made regular 11 aside football impossible.

During the decade clubroom had changed the purchase of some personal computers had meant that their use became popular with the boys and a further refurbishment of the BB room meant that they were supplemented by more games orientated machines such as play station 2's.

The summer of 2004 saw the under 14 football team travel to Scotland and narrowly lose their national title, the retention of the Daily Telegraph shield and yet another London Athletics title. However, for the first time since 1979 there was no camp. Camp had been arranged at Swanage but there was no take up from the boys and was thus cancelled. This highlighted the difficulties of a company section only approach, in that volume, in terms of either boys and staff are required to make it viable.

By the end of the year the company numbers were decidedly lop sided with some 40 boys on the roll after deducting 10 junior section boys a good recovery from the previous low numbers, the number of seniors was over 20. The company staff were faced with a difficult choice of going out and recruiting to add to a virtually non existent group or work with the large numbers of older boys whilst they had them .To try to do both with limited resources would have meant that neither would have got done. So the decision was made to work with the older boys.

2005 saw Kool drummings do two firsts . The first "first" was to go into a recording studio and produce a 17 track CD which, it has to be said, has sold well at subsequent public performances. The second was their first international performance or at least their first performance before a multi national crowd at the Baptist World Alliance in Birmingham where they played before a 10,000+

crowd from throughout the world both before and during the main evening performance. It is fair to say that they brought the house down.

Throughout this period the company chaplain was Alistair Clark who recalls the time in Birmingham amongst other activities from his time as Chaplain. " Parade services were a significant part of church life for most of my ministry. At my first one I realised what a change in mindset I needed to make: in Tooting the Dons were not Aberdeen Football Club! These services provided a very special opportunity for the young folk involved to discover and to develop their talents. It also gave them the chance to share in worship with others and to meet with the rest of the church family. The congregation certainly appreciated them. Unfortunately, it became impossible for the Brigades to continue to hold regular parade services.

Camps were a real highlight in the life of the Brigade - for the officers as well as the boys. A bold experiment was tried in our first summer: a joint camp with the Girls' Brigade Company! It was held at Ringmer, near Lewes, and was so successful that the pattern was followed for the next four years. For three years Audrey and I enjoyed the week under canvas sharing in camp life in all its rich variety. These were times of great fun and fellowship, with real opportunities for the youngsters to stretch themselves and try new experiences. I have particular memories of rock climbing, go-karting, paint-balling, swimming and cycling. Central to the camps was the challenge to the campers to follow Jesus as Saviour and Lord. These camps were amongst the most demanding periods of my ministry - trying to communicate relevantly and effectively was a huge, but exciting, challenge.

Kool Drummings held a very special place in the life of the brigade companies. The life of the church was greatly enriched by their participation in worship and at special events. Who could forget their joyous contribution to the Barbecue marking the Queen's Golden Jubilee? The steel band also played a significant role in the local community and far beyond being in great demand for all manner of occasions. They were received with great enthusiasm by eight thousand delegates from all over the world when they played at the

Centenary Assembly of the Baptist World Alliance. They excelled themselves!

The Company, ably led by its officers, and its band of volunteer helpers, played an important part in the life of the church. It reached out to many boys, influencing them by Christian teaching and example, and giving them opportunities to grow and develop into good and upright men. The influence on these boys and their families is incalculable. I know that the whole fellowship was profoundly grateful for all that the 70th did for "the advancement of Christ's kingdom among boys".

The company again had success at London level competition winning the basketball, Pr games, groundwork, cross country, senior five aside football and athletics. The latter win it has to be said was against very poor quality opposition and consequently the company decided that entering the event in future was meaningless. The result of these London victories was that the company won the Daily Telegraph shield for a third time and this was presented to the company by HRH the Duchess of Gloucester.

During 2005 a reunion was held which was remarkably well attended by almost 100 old boys from the 1920's through to 2004. At this event plans for the company centenary were unveiled.

Camp in 2005 involved four days in the new Forest staying at Burley . Twelve boys attended and the boys had a wide range of activities including water sports, paintball and Ice skating, devotions were led by the staff using a series of DVD's.

After camp 2005 a company institution ceased with the closure of bible class. The company staff decided with a heavy heart that the meeting was not serving its primary purpose as acting as a bridge into the church. Due to the fact that as soon as the boys were reaching 18 they were leaving and not coming back into the church. The church, somewhat surprisingly, didn't object or demure. In many respects the 70th were only belatedly and reluctantly catching up with most other BB companies who had closed bible class many years before and moving spiritual input to the normal meeting night and Sunday school or similar.

2006 saw the company again go through a transition year at the end of which the company numbers were reduced to below 30 which included a newly formed Amicus group for the over 18's. This was an attempt to keep in contact with those boys who were over the BB age limit and it has to be said has met with a relative degree of success. However within the company numbers were split between a dozen juniors and fifteen seniors and amicus boys and no eleven to fourteen year olds.

The senior boys returned to Northern Ireland in 2006 qualifying for the United Kingdom five aside finals in Belfast. They found a country considerably different to 1992 with peace declared. They also found a place where the BB was still well known to the extent that after the competition where we came 3rd, despite beating the winning team, we were able to visit the closed Stormont and Harland and Wolfe shipyards by our minibus driver using the magic words of "we've got some BB's from London can they come in and look around", acting like hey presto .We were able to drive in and see the grounds of the castle and the dry dock where the Titanic was built.

Later in the year the same age group entered the England and Wales Athletics championships held in Birmingham. Delayed by traffic we missed the first event and at the end of the day were announced as second place to the whole of the Birmingham battalion by 4 points, the boys shrugged that off saw England got knocked out of the World Cup and then enjoyed the following day at Alton Towers, and put the event down to experience. However, when the results were published a week or two later, lo and behold we weren't second but first as one our of wins had been left out of the total and so we won by 3 points. Our first belated victory!

During 2006 the company concentrated on the national events but still partook of some London competitions winning again the five a side football but handing over the Daily Telegraph shield to the 1st Enfield.

During 2006 Kool drummings concentrated on quality of appearances rather than quantity and one of their best received appearances was at a BB HQ garden party at Felden Lodge, which also yielded a good number of CD sales.

2007 was a strange year starting it with no company section boys and finishing with about a dozen who were able to win the London under 14 five aside football event. All the boys came without a formal recruiting event from contact with one ex junior section boy who brought along his friends from the estate. It has to be said that they are raw and starting from scratch means that's its almost like 1908 again except that then it was largely a new inexperienced staff staff group, now it's an older but more careworn staff with the same group of Chris Buss, Barry Green and Jim Ballard having been together for almost twenty years. Often using the text message rather than an absentee report to enquire of a boys whereabouts. A new badge scheme was introduced in 2007 and is much more a pick and mix version of things with drill largely sidelined which will surprise many a former member but the structure reflects modern life and the 21st century brigade with most companies doing most activities on the one night. The junior section numbers have again stayed at around a dozen and in many ways the programme is little changed from that of early years .The badge structure has again changed from the old achievement scheme but the activities in an evening are similar.

The senior section again reached the national five aside football finals, this time just a day trip to Wolverhampton and again despite beating the winners only made 3rd, a disappointment to the boys who with a couple of differences were the same group who had won the inaugural under 14 event in 2003 and were hoping to do the double. A few weeks earlier, however they did win the inaugural under 18 outdoor five aside football competition, and the company section were runners up in the under 14 event winning two penalty shoot outs to get there.

The company has changed over the past few years largely out of necessity but it has also survived so that at the time of writing it is able to enter its hundredth year and celebrate it's centenary. Something which other companies have not been able to do indeed of the 49 other companies that have existed in the Old South West

London Battalion area only one other reached a 100 -the 74th and non now exist with the closure of the 39th in September 2007.

The company in 2008 is in many ways at a crossroads, in it's centenary year. It has once again changed battalions now being part of Croydon battalion joining with some of the companies that made up the old South London Battalion way back in 1908.

The Brigade is in many ways different from that of 1908 in the same way that society is changed .The attitudes of boys are also different but they also reflect the society that they live in which is totally different to Edwardian England where the idea of play stations, TV's, computers, the internet, mobile phones and travel by air almost as a matter of routine would have been unheard of. Also the level of regulation that the officer of today has to work with from police checks, risk assessments and umpteen levels of training needed at least in the mind of the author acts as a disincentive to the prospective volunteer officer.

However the boys are still out there to be served .At the time of writing company numbers are up with some 20 boys in the company section and the new boys are enthusiastic even if a bit rough and ready, competition work is going well and plans are at an early stage for a weekend camp -under canvas for these boys and have just returned from Edinburgh narrowly failing to win yet another five a side final. This history is however about the past and thus plans for the future are for a future writer.

POST SCRIPT.   A Positive contribution….

It is difficult to assess the contribution that an organisation has had in terms of the difference it has made in the life of the community or in individuals. However despite this it is clear that the 70th London in its hundred years of individuals has impacted both on the local church and community, the BB as a wider body and most important-ly on the individual boys who have passed through its ranks.

With regard to the church at Tooting it is clear that generally the church has benefited from the existence of the Company. The Church has provided the officers to lead the company and the Company has in return provided leaders in the shape of deacons for the church. Three of the Company's captains have been deacons (Arthur Bowbeer, Neil Pheasant and Chris Buss), either during or after their captaincy whilst other officers who have served as dea-cons include George Alderman, Gordon Ferriman, Rolly Clark, Percy Sore and George Bartlett all of whom have been able to give greater wisdom to the deaconate from their experience with the boys and their families. This interplay between the role of BB officer and deacon shows the closeness of the relationship at most times between company and church, something that has not always been the case in many BB and church relationships . However as in most families tensions can be strained over the strangest of things as this correspondence from the mid 1950's concerning the use of the church kitchen shows

" Dear Mr Porter,
I am instructed by the deacons to write concerning the use of the Sunday School Kitchen….articles such as men's trousers, shorts, gloves, gym shoes and two very dirty lifeboy hats are among items recently found in the cupboard housing tea cloths and table cloths…. The deacons do not approve you having the use of the kitchen on Tuesday nights. The practice of officers changing in the kitchen is considered most unhygienic and objectionable.

Before reaching a decision regarding the use of the kitchen on Friday evenings, the deacons would like to know why it is necessary to have a Canteen at all bearing in mind that most of the lads will no doubt have had an adequate meal at home beforehand…We will consider this matter in the light of your reply .It is possible to say now, however that even if permission is finally given for you to use the kitchen on Fridays that permission will cover only the facilities needed to provide the canteen. Your use of the kitchen as a "battle" headquarters for the evening must cease."

Following a reply from Bert Porter and a visit to the deacons matters were resolved when the Church secretary wrote to Bert "Following our chat with you at the last deacon's meeting, I am asked to let you know that your application for the use of the kitchen on Tuesday and Friday evenings is approved."

It's interesting to note that the canteen has been served regularly until today's date and the kitchen is still used by the staff as HQ or refuge from the boys on meeting nights.

Although, the Company has been a major user of the church Premises since 1937, it has also made sure that the Church has benefited from it's presence whether through assisting with maintenance or the application of grant funding which the BB has obtained towards windows, boilers and roofs. Premises uses aside, relationships with the church have generally been a strong point within the company's history.

Whilst on the church, it is impossible not to comment on the Company's relationship with its sister organisation the 7th London Girls (Life) Brigade. The GLB started at Tooting in 1917 some nine years after the 70th. Although like the 70th early records are scant it is clear that there was a degree of social mixing outside of the company activities which in some cases led to life long relationships. There were also close staff links with the 7th of the five married 70th Captains, two of their wives became GB captains- Vera Bowbeer and Jenny Buss, two were GLB Lieutenants - Daphne Knights and Avis Porter, whilst Karen Pheasant actively assisted in the GB. The fact that often one was out one night and then the other was out on another night meant that it was often a case of literally meeting each other in the morning and sometimes at weekends !

The company has played a wider role within the wider church, it really isn't possible to list all of the former members who have become ministers, deacons, Sunday school teachers or just church members both at Tooting and elsewhere but the list runs well into three figures. However, no history of the company could be complete without mention of Owen Clark, the eldest son of Rolly and Ivy Clark, who after serving as boy and Life boy leader then spent some 40 years serving as a Baptist Missionary Society missionary in the Congo/Zaire. Owen when he was home from the mission field always had time for the company serving as camp chaplain on more than one occasion . He was also supported by the company both financially and in prayer support. The affection with which he was remembered was best measured by the large number of former members who attended his memorial service in 2006.

The 70th has also played a role in the wider Brigade movement providing at various times Battalion presidents, secretaries and treasurers, event convenors, district officials and even a member of the brigade executive. However, the company has also exported quite a long list of officers to other companies as the following non exhaustive list shows (Apologies in advance to those that have been missed off)

Fred Thomas -4th Thames Valley, later Captain 2nd Chislehurst
Pat Hodges -1st Blackwood
Tom Godfrey - Captain 126th London and Captain 138th London
Jack Mayhew - 9th Mid Surrey, Captain 1st Farnham
Les Wright - 7th Mid Surrey, Captain 3rd Mid Surrey
Les Collins- 1st Crawley
Percy Sore, 1st Barry, 14th London
Percy Alderman- Captain 7th East Surrey
Vic Sutton -Captain 7th Mid Surrey
Ewart Sutton-47th London, 1st East Surrey, Captain 1st Aston.
Ron Webb-7th Mid Surrey, Cardiff Battalion, Captain 14th Croydon
John Rowe-181st London
Graham Smith-11th Kingston & Merton
Bill Pizey-Captain 1st Emsworth
Alan Hemsley- Bognor Baptist Company.

Ray Holder-7th Mid Surrey
Harold Bennett-7th Mid Surrey.
Peter Ellis-1st Clwyd
Will Ward -17th Luton

The above list of ex 70th boys assisting companies elsewhere is impressive and Ron Webb gives one of the reasons as to why this was the case "One significant part of the 70th's achievements was its reputation for providing many officers to serve elsewhere. Soon after my return from the army in 1949. I joined the Old Boys association . At the outset it was expected that members should respond to assist the BB when called upon to do so. Within a few months I was assist- ing the 7th Mid-Surrey (Morden Baptist Church) as band master. Reg Lansdale a first class bugler in the 70th and later Ray Holder joined me. Harold Bennett, Vic Sutton and Les Wright all ex 70th were the principal officers in that Company. I stayed for about 10 years in which time we had won the Devonshire cup"

The above briefly describes the effect that the company has had on the church and the wider BB community. However it is surely amongst the boys who have passed through its ranks that it has been most effective. It is difficult for an outsider to judge how effective the Company has been in achieving its object that is "The advance- ment of Christ's Kingdom amongst boys and the promotion of habits of obedience reverence, discipline and Self respect and all that tends towards a true Christian manliness." but the best judges are the boys themselves and it is to them that we leave the final words some of which were written back in 1958 to answer the question of what did they gain from being in the 70th.

We have the following responses:-

Martin Nightingale: "A sense of self worth. Values for life, sound male models, many new skills and interests comradeship, valued friendships."

Arthur Bowbeer. "From my time in the company I gained an undy- ing bunch of friends but most of all I found Christ or He found me. My only regret is that I did not listen more in bible class."

Bob Sansome "Discipline and respect for my fellow beings, both of which helped me during National Service."

Peter Clark "I enjoyed my time in the company. I made many friends and learnt many useful things, as well as sharing in the esprit de corps . This all came in useful in later life as well as preparing me for National Service. In fact the first aid and drill gave me an advantage in joining the Royal Army Medical Corps."

Dillon Davies "I think I have gained what will be life long friendships with my peers of the time. I learnt how to work in a team, I also had to learn a lot of self discipline and restraint especially being around older boys who didn't care for back talk and such. From the staff I learnt about sacrifice and dedication without thought of reward."

Stephen Rock "I learned how to conduct my life and learnt good norms and values. It improved my leadership and communication skills which helps me during my life today. I learnt a lot about God and Christian beliefs.

Mark Palmer "I gained respect - we were the rabble really and the B.B. taught us to respect each other. It kept us off the streets and you will probably find that all the lads that were in our company are doing something good with their lives.

Neil Pheasant "The Lord Jesus Christ …. and more guidance for life and happy memories than I could ever write down!!

John Pizey "Even looking back I can see how it affected my outlook, what it did for me was taught me, discipline, the importance of teamwork, to show respect to others, how to take pride in all things.

It can be said the experience introduced me to the world of entertainment as I went on to learn to play the trumpet and trombone, in my spare time I fronted a band and became a part time entertainer, indeed I still perform at a small club in Australia, (not the trombone or trumpet now as health and teeth wont allow)
Prince Onyemachi "Other than what my sisters taught me through

life, almost everything that I have and almost everything that I am is down to all of the people associated with the BB."

Keith Holbrook " Friendship, fun self discipline and a great foundation for the life ahead. The BB leaves its mark on you, it makes its members stand out as people they've got qualities that are somehow lacking in other people."

Jack Fishpool " Discipline, smartness, value of friendship, timeliness and smartness."

Nathan Asare "it kept me off the streets and it stopped me from walking with bad crowds. It taught me how to conduct myself and it gave me some leadership skills.

Peter Ellis "A start into Christian life."

Michael Scott "I gained sporting prowess and religious education and making friends that I have to the current day."

Peter Knights "I Found Christ as my personal Saviour and Friend - character development."

Michael Wallace "Now a man in my sixties I know the influence the Officers and Company have had on my life and development of my personality."

John Ward "What the BB really did was set you standards for life, it was a standard or morals, a standard of ethics even if you didn't buy into the church and all that that was probably the most important thing the BB gave you."

Kobina Cooke ." The ability to do the things that were right and to make brave decisions."

Percy Sore. "I gained discipline, the love of God and the finest time of my life."

Bob Verrills." It gave us good standards, self respect and respect for others."

Brian Munro. "Discipline, teamwork and comradeship."

Bernard Shaw. "The way to play, play the game, sportsmanship and discipline."

W.Smith "It taught me to try and play the man under all circumstances in life."

G.Davison. "To be kind, courteous and considerate."

Ewart Sutton. "That discipline is needed in a boy's life and also the BB training was largely responsible for my deciding to follow Christ."

Vic Hopkins. "Loyalty to a cause, devotion to others and a rich comradeship."

George Alderman. ""The true value of real self discipline and a respect for the ideas and feelings of others."

Owen Clark. "Loyalty and Friendship."

Officers of the 70th London Company of the Boys' Brigade.

The list below contains a list of all those who have been enrolled as lieutenants, chaplains or captains of the company. It excludes life boy leaders who are listed separately

Name	Dates	Rank
William Cotsell	1908-1938	Captain
Rev.J Felmingham	1908-1911	Chaplain
Frank Taylor	1908	Lieut.
Ralph Harrup	1908-1911	Lieut.
Clifford Blazdell	1908-1910	Lieut.
Frederick Cotsell	1909-1915	Lieut.
Rev.Albert Veryard	1912-1917	Chaplain
George Alderman	1919-1928	Lieut.
Percy Alderman	1920-1933	Lieut
Harold Barrett	1920's	Lieut
Rev Fred H. King	1918-1933	Chaplain
Stanley Clarke	1922-1938	Lieut
Alan Wakeford	1927-1938	Lieut
Leslie Owens	1933-1938	Lieut
Rev. Andrew Wright	1934-1944	Chaplain
Herbert Porter	1938-1955	Captain
Jack Mayhew	1938-1942	Lieut
Roland Clark	1938-1967	Lieut
Christopher Nott	1938-1954	Lieut
William Webb	1942-1946	Lieut
Percy Sore	1945-52:1955-61	Lieut
Rev. Chris Parnell	1945-1951	Chaplain
Arthur (Tom) Godfrey	1946-1948	Lieut
Arthur Bowbeer	1946-1955	Lieut
	1955-1961	Captain
Gordon Ferriman	1946-1962	Lieut
Peter Knights	1951-56;1960-61	Lieut
	1961-1980	Captain
Rev. Edmund Gabb	1952-1961	Chaplain
Brian Flint	1956-1960	Lieut
Fred Bateman	1959-1970	Lieut

David Golder	1962-1966	Lieut
Rev Alan Hughes	1962-1968	Chaplain
Ralph Price	1965-1967	Lieut
Peter Ellis	1965-1970	Lieut
William Ward	1966-1967	Lieut
Michael Davis	1968-1977	Lieut
Brian Newman	1968-1971	Lieut
George Bartlett	1969-1983	Lieut
Rev. David Reddaway	1970-1977	Chaplain
Anthony Foard	1971-1972	Lieut
Neil Pheasant	1975-80;1984-89	Lieut
	1980-1984	Captain
Rev. Morrison Frew	1977-1984	Chaplain
James Ballard	1981-	Lieut
Keith Sylvester	1981-1982	Lieut
Christopher Buss	1982-1984	Lieut
	1984-	Captain
Rev Peter Taylor	1985-1992	Chaplain
Rev Brian Stevens	1993-1998	Chaplain
Barrington Green	1998-	Lieut
Rev Alistair Clark	2000-2006	Chaplain

From the formation of the Life boys in 1938 . Life boy leaders were separately registered with the Brigade. The list below shows all of the leaders of the 70th life boy team as registered with the Brigade.

Name	Dates
Marjorie Harding	1938-1939
Stanley Blake	1938-1939
Mrs Ivy Clark	1939-1964
Mrs Joan Godfrey	1946-1948
John Ward	1949-1954
Mrs Ethel Ward	1950-1954
Mrs Vera Bowbeer	1954-1966
Wiliam Ward	1956-1967
Owen Clark	1958-1960
Nigel Rigg	1958-1961
Barry Rowbotham	1962-1968
Alan Paramor	1964-1967
Graham Smith	1965-1966

Non Commissioned officers of the 70th London Company of the Boys' Brigade.

Under the regulations of the Boys' Brigade boys may be appointed to non commissioned officer ranks as either lance corporals, corporals, sergeants or staff sergeants. In addition adults over 18 may be appointed as staff sergeants or warrant officers. We have no records of NCO appointments before 1938, but the attached list by date order from 1938 is hopefully a complete record since that date. As records with regards to actual rank are not complete these have been omitted.

Name	Date.
Percy Sore	1935
Douglas Coole	1937
Reginald Worby	1937
Arthur Bowbeer	1937
Gordon Ferriman	1937
Eric Piddington	1938
Stanley Honeyman	1939
Leslie Wright	1941
Kenneth Collins	1941
Kenneth Marsh	1941
Frank Grimwood	1941
Peter Knights	1942
Leslie Mayo	1943
Ronald Webb	1943
Leonard Stacey	1943
Reginald Lansdale	1943
Frank Thompson	1943
Derek Coombs	1944
Harold Sporle	1944
Victor Burgess	1944
John Lemon	1945
Leonard Heath	1945
Raymond Drewitt	1945
Raymond Holder	1946

Douglas Strachan	1946
John Vidler	1946
Derek Lee	1947
Anthony Short	1947
Bernard Shaw	1948
Owen Clark	1948
Victor Earl	1948
Edgar Scammell	1948
Ronald Lang	1949
William Harris	1949
Alan Smith	1949
Brian Flint	1950
Peter Moore	1950
Kenneth Hill	1950
George Parsons	1950
Brian Rance	1950
George Fishpool	1951
Peter Clark	1951
Tony Stacey	1951
Peter Bryant	1951
Keith Holbrook	1952
Roy Challis	1952
Dennis Heath	1952
Gerald Rance	1952
Robert Sansome	1953
John Cook	1953
Ewart Clark	1953
Martin Nightingale	1953
Robert Bristow	1953
Terence Blumire	1954
Gordon Macpherson	1954
David Huddy	1954
Alan Bilyard	1954
David Blumire	1954
Brian Munro	1955
Robert Verrills	1955
Bernard Matcham	1956
Peter Essam	1956
David Golder	1956

Brian Shaw	1956
David Packman	1957
Ronald Sale	1957
Vincent Price	1957
John Ward	1957
Ronald Maxwell	1957
David Swallow	1958
Ralph Price	1958
Michael Allen	1958
Gordon Davis	1958
Richard Brown	1958
Barry Rowbotham	1959
John Fishpool	1959
David Shaw	1959
Alan Rance	1959
Colin Holton	1959
Peter Ellis	1959
William Ward	1960
Arnold Forty	1960
Michael Wallace	1960
Raymond Parker	1960
Albert King	1961
John Moore	1961
Brian Taylor	1961
John Rowe	1961
Alan Paramor	1962
Douglas Mills	1962
Roger Newman	1962
Michael Davis	1962
Martin Dennis	1962
Dennis Charman	1962
Michael Ellis	1962
Graham Smith	1962
Brian Newman	1963
John Gale	1963
Roy Norris	1963
Alan Taylor	1964
Dennis Loader	1964
Donald Feller	1964

Jim Boerio	1964
Leslie Beadle	1964
Graham Mountcastle	1964
Leighton.Taylor	1964
Alan Hubbard	1965
Colin Loader	1965
Martin Hughes	1965
Martin Richardson	1965
Michael Bartlett	1966
David Carmichael	1966
Anthony Foard	1966
Malcolm Harber	1966
William Gothard	1967
Chris.Mills	1967
Stamford Veitch	1967
Duncan Clark	1967
Alan Hemsley	1968
Neil Pheasant	1968
Paul Campbell	1969
Kevin Pheasant	1970
Chris Fry	1970
Trevor Jackson	1970
Lloyd Lilley	1971
M.English	1972
Vernon Sore	1972
Gary Peacock	1972
Raymond Kilsby	1973
Malcolm Sore	1974
Michael Frank	1975
Derek Ritchie	1975
Peter Judd	1976
Raymond Bachan	1976
Paul Parker	1977
Andre Belle	1977
Everald Irons	1980
Steven Ballard	1980
Carl Osborne	1980
Phillip Charles	1980
Chris Webb	1982

Andrew Johnson	1984
O'neil Howell	1985
Barrington Green	1985
Wendy Mcnab	1986
Paul Parris	1986
Daniel Sinclair	1986
Samuel Sinclair	1986
Denis Shattell	1986
Edmund Gonzales	1987
Freddie Adu	1987
Vusi Siphika	1988
Peter Williams	1989
Prince Onyemachi	1990
Nicholas Doyley	1990
Andrew Thomas	1990
Dean Hewitt-Reid	1990
Christopher Newlands	1991
Andrew Adu	1991
Jabbu Siphika	1991
Eze Nwatubi	1993
Giles Palmer	1993
Jason Hall	1994
Michael Scott	1994
Nathan Asare	1994
Paul D'Silveira	1995
Mark Palmer	1996
Dillon Davies	1996
Stephen Blackwood	1996
Daniel Buss	2001
Wilfred Rockliffe	2002

Company Numbers.

The table below is based on the returns to Brigade Headquarters.
Company and senior section boys are grouped under one heading .
Before 1966 junior section was life boy team. No life boy records
exist before 1950.

Year	Company
1909	31
1910	35
1911	33
1912	32
1913	42
1914	32
1915	36
1916	30
1917	27
1918	27
1919	50
1920	43
1921	41
1922	33
1923	44
1924	36
1925	31
1926	38
1927	45
1928	34
1929	30
1930	22
1931	27
1932	43
1933	26
1934	25
1935	27
1936	31
1937	21
1938	32

1939	33	
1940	24	
1941	37	
1942	34	
1943	40	
1944	38	
1945	39	
1946	39	
1947	39	
1948	51	
1949	55	
1950	51	
1951	61	

	Company/ Seniors	Lifeboys/ Juniors
1952	70	28
1953	60	32
1954	64	18
1955	57	19
1956	56	18
1957	43	30
1958	49	34
1959	59	37
1960	59	36
1961	57	25
1962	46	24
1963	43	17
1964	47	26
1965	40	28
1966	39	24
1967	33	33
1968	36	38
1969	39	28
1970	24	18
1971	18	35
1972	27	32

Company/ Seniors		Lifeboys/ Juniors
1973	20	34
1974	26	21
1975	17	25
1976	22	18
1977	30	20
1978	30	19
1979	21	18
1980	15	17
1981	16	12
1982	16	12
1983	20	11
1984	15	13
1985	19	13
1986	24	10
1987	28	11
1988	26	12
1989	25	13
1990	24	15
1991	24	17
1992	30	17
1993	33	16
1994	41	16
1995	36	19
1996	41	21
1997	45	10
1998	44	12
1999	38	12
2000	28	10
2001	28	7
2002	28	10
2003	28	5
2004	27	3
2005	23	5
2006	17*	12
2007	28*	13

* includes Amicus group

Competition Successes -

National Competitions-UK

Five a side football (under 18): Winners 1993,1997, 2001,
Runners up 1990, 1995, 2008.
Finalists 1988, 1991,1992,1994,2000,2006,2007

Five a side football (under 14) Winners 2003
Runners up 2004

Volleyball: Finalists 1986,1987, 1988,1989,1990,1991,1992,1993

Table Tennis: Finalists 1988

Badminton: Finalists 1998, 2002:

ENGLAND & WALES
Athletics : - Senior Winners 2006
Five a side football -Outdoor Under 14 Winners 2002, Runners up
2003,2007
Five a side football -Outdoor under 18 Winners 2007
Ten pin bowling -Finalists (4th)- 1994

London Competitions:

Daily Telegraph Shield 2003,2004,2005

Eleven a side cricket:
1986,1989,1990,1991,1992,1993,1994,1997,1998,1999
Six a side cricket: 1987,1989,1991,1995,1997,1999.2001,2002

First Aid: 1962,1963,1965,1966,1967

Junior section football 1998,2001

Vaulting & groundwork: 1967

Gymnastics; 1965,1966,1967

Vaulting: 1997,1998, 2002

Groundwork: 1992,1998,1999,2001,2004,2005

Parallel bars: 1987,1988,1989,1992

Physical recreation:
1986,1988,1989,1992,1993,1996,1999,2003/4,2004/5,

Under 14 cross- country: 1995,1996,2001,2005
Open cross country 2003

Over 14 five a side football:
1992,1993,1994,1995,1996,1997,1998,1999,2000,2001,2002,2005,
2006

Under 14 five a side football:
1987,1990,1994,1995,1997,2001,2004,2008

Athletics 2002,2003,2004,2005

Basketball 2000,2001,2003 2003/4,2004/5,

South London, South West London or Wandsworth Battalion

Note all years reflect end of session so 1943 is session 1942/43

1943- First aid
1944- Barnsley Colours
1945- First aid
1946- PT, First Aid
1950 - Cricket, Band
1953- First aid; Band
1954-Bugle team
1955-Band; 2nd division football
1956-Bband
1957- Junior football cup ; athletics, cricket
1958-Cricket (junior & senior), athletics, band, first aid
1959-Athletics, band, first aid.
1960-Athletics, first aid, Junior football
1961-Band, bugle team, athletics, first aid
1962- First aid, athletics
1963-First aid, athletics
1964-gym,first aid, band, drill "b" competition
1965 bugle team, first aid, gym, groundwork, athletics
1966- cross country, first aid, vaulting & groundwork, gymnastics
1967- first aid, vaulting & groundwork, gymnastics
1969-athletics, squad drill
1971- junior football
1982-Pr games
1983-Vaulting, groundwork
1984- Vaulting ; athletics
1985 senior football, pr games, vaulting,groundwork; athletics; Six a side cricket
1986-Cross country, vaulting, groundwork, Pr games, bugle team, six a side cricket u18,u14; athletics; Alan Noon Colour, cricket, junior football, squad drill
1987 -Senior football, junior football, six a side cricket u18,u14, u14 five aside, Pr games, groundwork, cross country; athletics
1988- u14 five aside football;vaulting, groundwork, six a side cricket u18,u14; pr games; athletics, football
1989- six a side cricket u18,u14, u14 five aside; pr games ; vaulting,

groundwork; athletics, table tennis, squad drill, swimming gala

1990 pr games athletics

1991 u14 five aside, athletics, scripture-hons cup

1992 u14 five aside, athletics, scripture-hons cup;

pr games; table tennis ;

1993 u14 five aside, athletics, scripture-hons cup; scripture

1994 u14 five aside, athletics, scripture-hons cup; scripture

1995- u14 five aside, athletics

1996-swimming gala; athletics

1997- u14 five aside; swimming gala

1998-Swimming gala

1999- u14 five aside

2000-Swimming gala

2001- u14 five aside

2002- u14 five aside

Other Competitions

1952- Roberts Shield- Band
1958- Wandsworth district youth sports - senior and junior boys trophy.
1992 -Under 12 & under 14 West Kent Churches football 3League & cup
1993- L B Wandsworth /Metropolitan Police under 17 Five a side football
1994- Under 12 & Under 14 West Kent Churches football League & cup
1995- LB.Merton -Youth basketball championship
1996- Croydon Battalion -under 14 cross country
1998- Under 15 West London -football league
1999- Under 15 West London -football league; West London Under 18 five aside
2000- West London Battalion under 18 five aside; Reading Stedfast Association under 16 & over 16 five aside football
2001- West London Battalion under 18 five aside
2002- West London Battalion under 14 and under18 five aside; Bromley Battalion Football league & cup
2003- Bromley Battalion Football league & cup
2004- Bromley Battalion Cup, Kingston Merton & Mid Surrey under 14 five aside and under 18 five aside
2005- Kingston Merton & Mid Surrey under 18 five aside; athletics
2006- Kingston Merton & Mid Surrey under 18 five aside
2008- Kingston Merton & Mid Surrey under 14 five aside. Croydon Battalion- under 14 five a side, under 18 five a side.

Various dates :St Johns First aid competitions.

2004 and 2007 Wandsworth Youth Group of the year.

Terminology.

A beginners guide to some of the terminology used within the Boys'
Brigade over the past 100 years.

BB STRUCTURE
Company: The basic unit of the Boys' Brigade .Each company is
part of a church. Prior to September 1965 where the term company
is used, it refers to the 12-17 year old group. Post 1965 it refers to
all ages.

Battalion. The local area grouping of BB companies. Battalions are
used for various activities but with particular relevance to the boys
organise competitive events

District. The geographical area above battalion. Throughout it's life
the 70th has been in the London district.

BB COMPANY STRUCTURE

Boy reserves. The name for the group for 8-12 year olds operated
from 1918 until the 1930's

Lifeboys . Name given to 8-11 year old boys between 1938 and
1965. Operated as a distinct group within the umbrella of the Boys'
Brigade.

Anchor boys. Under 8's group operated from 1977-1985, prior to
1977 called Blue imps.

Junior section. From 1965 the title given to the 8-11 year old group.

Company Section. From 1965 the title given to the 11-15 year age
group.

Senior section. From 1965 the title given to the 15-18 year age
group.

BB RANKS

Captain. The officer responsible for the overall operation of the BB company.

Lieutenant. An officer who has completed full BB training.

Warrant Officer. A member of staff who is in training to be an officer or for other reasons having completed training does not wish to be considered for the rank of Lieutenant

All officers in the ranks above are recommended for appointment by the church to which the BB company is attached and this is then ratified by the Battalion and the Brigade at National level

NCO's. There are four ranks which a boy may be promoted to these are lance corporal, corporal, sergeant and staff sergeant each of which have are designated by the wearing of stripes or chevrons. Lance corporal is the lowest rank with one stripe rising to staff sergeant with four. NCO's are appointed by the captain

Private: The rank of any boy member of the Company before 1965 or the company section after 1965 who was not an NCO.

BB YEAR.

The BB year runs from 1st September to 31st August and is often referred to as the session. The age limit for instance is measured by the session and thus a Boy will reach the age limit not on his 18th birthday but at the 31st August on or after his 18th birthday.